ANOTHER INCONVENIENT TRUTH 2

Defending Young Earth Creationism

Justin Derby

ISBN: 978-0-9862430-2-8

Endorsements

"Derby provides brave and bold opposition to the compromising positions of leading apologists such as William Lane Craig, Hugh Ross, Frank Turek, John Lennox, and Mike Licona who hold that Genesis is compatible with an old earth."

-Jay Hall M.S. Assistant Math Professor, Howard College

"The reader will learn about what is going on in the online podcast, social media, and video sharing platforms. These platforms are where many of the youth of today get their understanding of truth. In his book, Justin explains some very frightening goings on and makes recommendations for how to combat these things. I would say that Justin has an online expertise, developed from a number of years of experience that is certainly beyond mine; and I believe beyond that of many other more mature creationist researchers, writers, and speakers. He clearly explains how and why so many young people are being influenced to reject

the Bible and run away from the Church...Overall, I highly recommend this book to anyone interested in the origins controversy and associated Christian issues."

-J.D. Mitchell. P.E., MBS, Founder of Creation Engineering Concepts

Endorsements For *Another Inconvenient Truth*:

"With wisdom well past his years, and with dogged determination, Justin goes right at the pressing issues of our day, with an unwavering commitment to the unchanging inerrant Word of God. True lovers of truth will find this book extremely helpful."

-Dr. Jim Jenkins, Founder of The Jude 3 Fellowship, and author of "Fatal Drift: Is The Church Losing it's Anchor?"

"For those of my readers that know me personally and want to know why I'd promote a book that goes against some of my personal views on my blog, the answer is simple. The book offers a wealth of information that supports its arguments. If you want to understand some of the current unpopular Christian arguments in the United States, this is a great book to pick up, no matter which side you are on."

-Theresa Neal, New Inkling's Writing Blog

"I don't personally agree with everything that the author says in the book, but I really enjoyed it because Justin Derby puts forward such a strong argument, in a very intelligent and articulate fashion. I found myself admiring him for having the courage to defend his beliefs in areas that are controversial to say the least!

Read this book with an open mind; I guarantee that it will prove to be extremely thought provoking!"

-Lesley H., Amazon Reviewer

Table of Contents

Acknowledgments

I would like to thank my mom and dad for giving me a solid starting foundation for my faith when I was growing up.

I would like to thank Dr. Jim Jenkins for faithfully preaching the Word of God for all those years that he was my pastor at the Cottage Grove Faith Center, and for showing me that writing an apologetics book in defense of the Christian faith was something that could be done.

I would like to thank JD Mitchell, Milt Marcy, Jay Hall, and Dr. Johnson C Philip for not only helping review and edit this book, but also for giving me the inspiration and courage to make a book about young earth creationism.

I would like to thank other young earth creationists like Dr. Thomas Kindell, Mike Riddle, Chris Ashcraft, etc for paving the way for younger creationists like myself to bring the truth about reality and origins to the world.

Lastly, I want to thank Jesus for giving us a way out of what we have coming to us for our crimes against God, and for taking me on this years-long journey to understand the truth about reality. If it wasn't for Jesus showing me the truth about origins and working on me over the years, this book would never have been written.

Introduction

It seems like it has been a lifetime since I wrote *Another Inconvenient Truth*.

My ministry, *Truth: The Objective Reality* (TTOR), has also seen big changes since then.

Back when I wrote *Another Inconvenient Truth* over the course of the spring, summer, and fall of 2014, TTOR existed only as a blog on blogspot.com. There was no YouTube channel for TTOR, and I was using primarily Facebook to promote the one or two blog posts I would post each month. My audience was so small that it was essentially non-existent.

Flash forward to 2021, and things have progressed rapidly; the mass censorship of conservative and religious content creators on the mainstream social media tech giants like YouTube, Twitter, Facebook, and Instagram has progressed so much that TTOR has become a multi-platform online ministry out of necessity, taking full advantage of the alternative technology (alt-tech) social media platforms that have emerged in recent years such as JoshWho TV, UGETube,

NewTube, Loop, Pocketnet, USA.Life, BitChute, Gab, Minds, etc. I even launched my own open-source alt-tech alternative to Facebook called Creation Social on December 26, 2020.

But there was something else that happened shortly before I started writing *Another Inconvenient Truth* that would end up changing my life forever. In 2014, Bill Nye debated Ken Ham at the Creation Museum over whether or not creation was a viable model in a debate that was live-streamed on YouTube, and has been viewed roughly seven million times to date. Prior to this debate, I was an old earth creationist, and although I was aware that there was a creationism position called young earth creationism, I didn't really know much about it because I had never studied young earth creationist materials.

It was when I was watching Ken Ham debate Bill Nye in 2014 that I was finally exposed to the young earth creationism position and what it taught. After I saw the debate, I went to the websites of young earth creationist ministries like Answers in Genesis (AiG) and the Institute for Creation Research (ICR), and I encountered all of the scriptural arguments that these ministries were using to show that the Bible clearly taught that the earth and universe are roughly 6,000 years old. I went to the references that these ministries provided to prove that the Bible taught a 6,000 year-old earth and universe, and I also checked the context around the references to make sure that ministries like AiG and ICR were accurately representing what the scriptures teach. What I found is that the scriptural arguments that young earth creationists made were irrefutable.

Despite the fact that the scriptural arguments for young earth creationism's timeline of history were irrefutable, and despite the fact that sound scriptural arguments are normally enough to convince me that the Bible teaches something, I did not immediately convert to being a young earth creationist. At this time, I was not able to leave old earth creationism behind because I was attracted to the personalities and credentials of old earth creationist authority figures like William Lane Craig, Frank Turek, John Lennox, and Mike Licona. I looked at the academic credentials and accolades that these guys had, I looked at the seemingly Godly lives they were living, and I thought to myself, "there's no way that these guys could be so fundamentally wrong about what the Bible says about origins; they seem to have such a high view of the scriptures."

I thought that old earth creationist authority figures had a high view of scripture because they insisted over and over again that they did, but everything changed in the fall of 2014 when I came across a 2000 debate between progressive creationist Hugh Ross and young earth creationist Kent Hovind. In this debate, there came a point where Kent Hovind and Hugh Ross were debating over the fourth day of creation, and at one point, Hugh Ross said that the sun, moon, and stars were not actually created on the fourth day of creation. Hugh Ross claimed that the sun, moon, and stars had already been created prior to the fourth day of creation, but that they were obscured by a non-transparent atmosphere, and on the fourth day of creation when it appeared to the observer on the surface of the earth that the sun, moon, and stars were being created, what actually happened was that the atmosphere became transparent on the fourth day of creation, and the sun, moon, and stars became visible for the first time.

That's right, folks; you're reading that correctly. In order to deny the straightforward reading of the creation account regarding the fourth day of creation, Hugh Ross literally said that the observer on the surface of the earth did not know what they were looking at when the sun, moon, and stars were being created on the fourth day of creation. Since the observer on the surface of the earth was God, Hugh Ross is saying that God did not know what he was looking at when he was creating the sun, moon, and stars on the fourth day of creation!

After I watched Hugh Ross say that, I instantly realized the Hugh Ross not only had an incredibly low view of scripture, but that he also viewed the opinions of fallible, god-hating men as a higher authority than God himself, at least on the issue of origins. Since most old earth creationist authority figures that I followed refer to Hugh Ross in their own works and they make the same kinds of scriptural arguments as Hugh Ross, I came to understand the truth about old earth creationists, which is that God and the Bible are not the ultimate authority over every aspect of their lives.

As we go through this book together, I will show how the Bible teaches a 6,000 year-old earth and universe as well as show evidence from science that supports a 6,000 year-old earth and universe. I will not only expose the religious nature of the evolutionary atheistic worldview and the fruit that comes from it, but I will also expose the compromised and heretical nature of old earth creationism, and the effect it can have on those who call themselves followers of Jesus.

In case you haven't noticed, the culture and information war in the western world rages on more fiercely than ever before. The big billion-dollar tech corporations like YouTube, Facebook, and Twitter think that they are above all laws and beyond any accountability as they try to rig elections and silence all dissidents; the Marxists have successfully turned the American education system into an indoctrination center for socialism, and the globalists are more boldly and publicly than ever pushing for the creation of a New World Order. You cannot understand how these authoritarians took over our society and world unless you understand the creation versus evolution debate.

Young earth creationism is the hill to die on for a follower of Jesus.

It's time to defend the hill.

Chapter 1

Young Earth Creationism

Defining Terms

In order to give a proper defense of young earth creationism, it is important to know exactly what we're talking about when we talk about young earth creationism. Therefore, we need to define what young earth creationism is, and what a young earth creationist is.

To put it simply, young earth creationism is the claim that God created the universe, the earth, the sea, and everything that is in those three things over the course of six ordinary days roughly 6,000 years ago. As we will see later in this chapter, this definition comes from a straight-forward contextual reading of the Bible. We will also see in chapter two that the concept of the earth and universe being billions of years old comes from a complete rejection of the Bible's explanation of origins.

Therefore, a young earth creationist is a person who believes in young earth creationism.

Where Does The Bible Say God Made Everything In Six Days?

So now that we know what young earth creationism is, and what young earth creationists are, we have to ask: On what basis do young earth creationists make these claims? What is young earth creationism based on?

The answer, of course, is the Bible.

The reason that young earth creationists claim that God created the universe, the earth, the sea, and everything that is in them over the course of six days is because God himself literally said so:

Exodus 20:8-11: *"Remember the Sabbath day by keeping it holy. Six days you shall labor and do all your work, but the seventh day is a sabbath to the Lord your God. On it you shall not do any work, neither you, nor your son or daughter, nor your male or female servant, nor your animals, nor any foreigner residing in your towns. For in six days the Lord made the heavens and the earth, the sea, and all that is in them, but he rested on the seventh day. Therefore the Lord blessed the Sabbath day and made it holy."*

In case he wasn't clear enough the first time, God reiterates later on in Exodus that he made the universe and the earth in six days:

Exodus 31:12-17: *"Then the Lord said to Moses, 'Say to the Israelites, "You must observe my Sabbaths. This will be a sign between me and you for the generations to come, so you may know that I am the Lord, who makes you holy.*

Observe the Sabbath, because it is holy to you. Anyone who desecrates it is to be put to death; those who do any work on that day must be cut off from their people. For six days work is to be done, but the seventh day is a day of sabbath rest, holy to the Lord. Whoever does any work on the Sabbath day is to be put to death. The Israelites are to observe the Sabbath, celebrating it for the generations to come as a lasting covenant. It will be a sign between me and the Israelites forever, for in six days the Lord made the heavens and the earth, and on the seventh day he rested and was refreshed.""'

As we can see in these two passages from Exodus, God is saying that he made the universe, the earth, the sea, and everything that is in them over the course of six ordinary days like we experience today. The reason why we know that this is what these passages are saying is that in both passages, God precedes this by saying that the Israelites are to work six days and rest on the seventh.

When God tells the Israelites to work six days and rest on the seventh, he is clearly referring to the seven-day work week that we live through today. So when God tells the Israelites that they are to work six days and rest on the seventh because he created everything in six days and rested on the seventh, God is not only showing us that the days of creation were ordinary days like we experience today, but he is clearly telling the Israelites to do something that he himself did, which is work six days and rest on the seventh.

Where Does The Number 6,000 Come From?

At this point, you may be thinking to yourself, "Ok, I see why young earth creationism teaches that the universe, earth, sea, and everything in those three things were created by God over six ordinary days like we experience today, but where do young earth creationists get the idea that the universe and earth were created 6,000 years ago?"

The answer to that question is, once again, the Bible.

One of the arguments that non-believers and old earth creationists like to bring against young earth creationism is that there is no specific verse or passage that specifically says "the universe and earth are 6,000 years old", or "and thus saith the Lord, 'I made the universe and earth 6,000 years ago'".

While this is technically true, the argument is asinine because: 1) young earth creationism has never claimed such a thing, and 2) the Bible itself gives us all the necessary data to come to the conclusion that it teaches that the earth and universe are 6,000 years old.

What data, you ask?

According to the Bible, God created Adam on the sixth day of creation. When Adam was 130, he had a son named Seth (Genesis 5:3). When Seth was 105, he had a son named Enosh (Genesis 5:6). When Enosh was 90, he had a son named Kenan (Genesis 5:9). When Kenan was 70, he had a son named Mahalalel (Genesis 5:12). When Mahalalel was 65, he had a son named Jared (Genesis 5:15). When Jared was 162, he had a son named Enoch (Genesis 5:18). When Enoch was 65, he had a son named Methuselah (Genesis 5:21). When Methuselah was 187, he had a son named Lamech (Genesis

5:25). When Lamech was 182, he had Noah (Genesis 5:28). When Noah was 500, he had sons named Shem, Ham, and Japheth (Genesis 5:32).

Noah was 600 years old when the flood happened (Genesis 6:6), which means that 100 years had passed between when God warned him about it, and when it actually happened. According to Genesis 8:13, Noah was 601 when the water from the flood had completely receded. According to Genesis 11:10, Shem became the father of Arphaxad two years after the flood. When Arphaxad was 35, he became the father of Shelah (Genesis 11:12). When Shelah was 30, he had a son named Eber (Genesis 11:14). When Eber was 34, he had a son named Peleg (Genesis 11:16). When Peleg was 30, he had a son named Reu (Genesis 11:18). When Reu was 32, he had a son named Serug (Genesis 11:20). When Serug was 30, he had a son named Nahor (Genesis 11:22). When Nahor was 29, he had a son named Terah (Genesis 11:24). When Terah was 70, he had Abram, Nahor (a different one), and Haran (Genesis 11:26). When Abram was 100, he had Isaac (Genesis 21:5). When Isaac was 60 years old, Jacob and Esau were born (Genesis 25:24-26). When Jacob was 130 years old, he and the rest of the Israelites moved to the region of Goshen in Egypt (Genesis 47:27-28).

When you add all those numbers together, we can see

that 2,239 years passed between the creation of Adam, and when Jacob and the Israelites moved to Egypt.

In Exodus 12:40, we read the following:

"Now the length of time the Israelite people lived in Egypt was 430 years."

In other words, 430 years passed between Jacob and the Israelites moving to Egypt, and the actual Exodus from Egypt.

In 1 Kings 6:1, we read the following:

"In the four hundred and eightieth year after the Israelites came out of Egypt, in the fourth year of Solomon's reign over Israel, in the month of Ziv, the second month, he began to build the temple of the Lord."

In other words, the exodus to the fourth year of King Solomon's reign was 480 years.

The fourth year of king Solomon's reign was 966 BC, and Jesus was born in 4 BC, so the time between the fourth year of king Solomon's reign and the birth of Jesus was 962 years.

Since this is the year 2020, and since our calendar starts at the birth of Jesus, this means that 2,020 years have passed since Jesus was born.

Now that we have all the data to determine the age of the earth and universe, we simply need to add all the numbers together: 2,239 + 430 + 480 + 962 +2,020

When you add all that up, we find that the universe and the earth are both 6,131 years old. Most young earth creationists round it down to 6,000 years in order to make it simple for the sake of argumentation.

ARE THE CREATION DAYS REALLY 24-HOUR PERIODS OF TIME?

At this juncture, you may have noticed that I used Exodus 20:8-11 to interpret how long the creation days in Genesis 1:1-2:3 are. The reason why I do that is because old earth creationists like to isolate the creation account from the rest of the scriptures before they twist and manipulate the creation account to make you think that the days of creation are not ordinary days like we experience today.

So why do most young earth creationists believe that

the days in the creation account are 24-hour periods of time like we experience today?

The answer is that most Hebrew scholars say that the author of Genesis 1:1-2:3 intended the days of creation to be understood as 24-hour days, and the language of the creation account makes it clear that the days cannot be anything but ordinary days like we experience today.

In a letter that he wrote to David C. C. Watson back in 1984, James Barr, a Regius Professor of Hebrew at Oxford University, said the following:

"So far as I know, there is no professor of Hebrew or Old Testament at any world-class university who does not believe that the writer(s) of Gen. 1–11 intended to convey to their readers the ideas that (a) creation took place in a series of six days which were the same as the days of 24 hours we now experience (b) the figures contained in the Genesis genealogies provided by simple addition a chronology from the beginning of the world up to later stages in the biblical story, Noah's Flood was understood to be world-wide and extinguish all human and animal life except for those in the ark." (1)

In a 2012 article titled "24 Hours-Plain As Day" on the

Answers in Genesis website, Dr. Jud Davis, an associate professor of Greek at Bryan College, wrote the following:

"I wondered what modern "world-class" Hebraists would say about Barr's statement today, so I tracked down several leading experts to ask their opinion.

Hugh Williamson is the current Regius Professor of Hebrew at Oxford University. Oxford is perhaps the most prestigious university in the world, and Williamson is one of the top Hebraists anywhere. In an email he responded, 'So far as the days of Genesis 1 are concerned, I am sure that Professor Barr was correct. . . . I have not met any Hebrew professors who had the slightest doubt about this unless they were already committed to some alternative by other considerations that do not arise from a straightforward reading of the Hebrew text as it stands.'

I also emailed Barr's letter to Emanuel Tov of Hebrew University Jerusalem; he would be on anyone's list of Hebrew experts. Professor Tov responded in kind: 'For the biblical people this was history, difficult as it is for us to accept this view.' Here was confirmation from a Jewish man who spoke and thought in Hebrew.

There is a residential theological research library called Tyndale House, located outside of Cambridge University in England. You can rent a room and literally live in the library. It is perhaps the best such facility in the world. During its history some of the top scholars have been its 'warden.' The current warden is a young man of encyclopedic knowledge named Peter Williams. He sent a paper to me that said, 'Although the Young Universe Creationist position is not widely held within secular academia, the position—that the author of Genesis 1 maintained that the world was created in six literal days—is nearly universally held.'

I could go on, listing dozens and dozens of names, but there is no need. The scholarship is clear. The writer of Genesis 1–2 meant the text to teach chronology in terms of normal days. So why would almost the entirety of evangelical scholarship reject the author's intent?" (2)

As you can see, there is very little doubt among Hebrew scholars that the author of the creation account intended the days of creation to be understood as ordinary days like we experience today. That being said, we do not need the say-so of academic authority figures to conclude that the days of creation in Genesis 1:1-2:3 are ordinary days like we experience today; we simply have to believe the straight-forward and contextual reading of the text itself.

The Hebrew word that is used for "day" in the creation account is *yom*. *Yom* has multiple meanings, one of them being a period of time longer than 24-hours, and old earth creationists will assert that because the word *Yom* has multiple definitions, there's no way that the days of creation are ordinary days like we experience today. Unfortunately for them, it is the context around the word *Yom* that determines which definition of the word applies.

As Todd Friel, the main host of Wretched TV/Radio, pointed out on page 155 in his book *Judge Not* in a chapter called "Compromising On Creation":

"It is an inviolable Hebrew rule of grammar that whenever a number appears before the word Yom, *it always means a single twenty-four-hour day. Always. Each time. No exceptions. God seems to belabor the point in Genesis 1 by placing a number before each of the seven days of creation: first day, second day, third day, etc. This cannot mean 'the first long age,' etc."*

Todd Friel is absolutely correct; when you look at Genesis 1:5, 1:8, 1:13, 1:19, 1:23, 1:31, and 2:2-3, you clearly see a number attached to each of the creation days. This alone proves that the days of creation were ordinary days like we experience today, but there is one other thing that God put in the creation account that rules out the possibility of the creation days being anything other than ordinary days like we experience today.

In each of the first six verses that I quoted above, the phrase "And there was evening, and there was morning" is attached to the word "day" along with a number:

Genesis 1:5: *"God called the light 'day,' and the darkness he called 'night.' And there was evening, and there was morning—the first day."*

Genesis 1:8: *"God called the vault 'sky.' And there was evening, and there was morning—the second day."*

Genesis 1:13: *"And there was evening, and there was morning—the third day."*

Genesis 1:19: *"And there was evening, and there was morning—the fourth day."*

Genesis 1:23: *"And there was evening, and there was morning—the fifth day."*

Genesis 1:31: *"God saw all that he had made, and it was very good. And there was evening, and there was morning—the sixth day."*

As we can see with each of the first six days of creation, the phrase "And there was evening, and there was morning", as well as a number, was attached to the word "day". And since both the phrase "And there was evening, and there was morning" and a number are attached to the word "day" in these verses, there is absolutely no way that these days are anything other than ordinary days like today; to insist that they aren't in light of these two things requires us to throw out everything we know about how language works.

At this point, you have probably noticed that I have been saying that the days of creation were ordinary days like we experience today instead of saying that they were 24-hour days like we experience today like *Answers In Genesis* and other creationist ministries say. There's a reason for that.

I used to say that the days of creation were 24-hour days like we experience today, but then I came across a fellow young earth creationist named Dr. Troy Lawrence who offered an interesting theory about how long the days of creation were on page 100 of his book *Origins*:

"In the beginning, on the first day of creation, when God started rotating the formless mass of water and dirt that was to be earth, that rotational speed was faster than the current rotational speed of the earth. This means that the evening and morning of the first day occurred slightly faster and in shorter time than the current 24 hours it takes for one rotation of the earth.

How do we know this? The moon is one reason we know this for certain. The moon's gravity takes angular momentum away from the earth's rotational velocity, and the moon uses the captured energy to move away from the earth at 1.5 inches per year. Each ocean tide, twice a day, is caused by the moon's gravity. Each time the ocean tides occur, angular momentum is taken out of the earth's rotational velocity. This is to say that the moon is slowing the earth down by means of gravity. It is important to note that the moon uses this energy to move away from the earth.

Since the moon is moving away from the earth at 1.5 inches per year, it's logical to presume that the moon was closer to the earth in past millennia. And when the moon was closer to the earth, the moon's gravitational pull would have had a greater effect on the earth's ocean tides. With greater oceans tides, more angular momentum was taken out of the *earth's spin. The more angular momentum taken out of the earth's spin, the greater the reduction in the earth's spin.*

Therefore, when the moon was closer to the earth, the moon slowed the spin of the earth to a greater degree. Putting all the pieces together, we discern that the earth spun faster in past millennia.

With a faster spinning earth, the length of on day was shorter. This begs the question: 'How long was a day when dinosaurs roamed the earth?'

Currently, the earth is slowing 2 milliseconds per 100 years. But this rate of reduction of speed is not constant. In prior centuries, the rate of reduction would be larger. Why? Because the moon would have been closer and its gravitational pull would have caused greater ocean tides, which would have taken more speed out of the spinning earth. The further back in time we go, the greater reduction of spin exponentially. In addition, large asteroid impacts would have reduced the earth's spin velocity. Also, when large asteroids hit the earth to initiate the flood and the breakup of Pangaea, the large tectonic plate movements would have also taken away angular momentum from the earth's spin. Putting these pieces of the puzzle together, an estimate for the length of day at the time of Adam and Eve, some 6,000 years ago, would be approximately 15-17 hours long." (4)

According to Dr. Lawrence, the days of creation were probably 15-17 hours long because the moon would have been much closer to the earth back then than it is now, which would cause the earth's rotation speed to go up to the point where it would take 15-17 hours to make one full rotation instead of 24 hours.

I do not fully believe in Dr. Lawrence's theory, but his theory has some plausibility to it, and because it has some plausibility to it, I put his theory about the days of creation being 15-17 hours long on the table as a possibility for the length of the creation days. Allowing for the possibility of the days of creation being shorter than 24 hours does absolutely nothing to aid the cause of atheists, evolutionists, and old earth creationists, so I don't see any harm in entertaining the idea as a possibility, even if I do not fully believe it.

Whether the days of creation were 15-17 hours long due to the earth's spin being faster, or were 24-hour days like we experience today, I don't lean too heavily towards either one because there is zero doubt based off the text of the creation account and passages like Exodus 20:8-11 and Exodus 31:12-17 that the days of creation were ordinary days like we experience today.

SCIENTIFIC EVIDENCE SUPPORTING YOUNG EARTH CREATIONISM

What scientific evidence is there supporting young earth creationism? In this section, we will look at fundamental scientific laws that everyone agrees on that were described by the scriptures thousands of years in advance, the same scriptures that teach that the earth and universe are 6,000 years old.

The first one is the second law of thermodynamics. While the first law of thermodynamics states that there is a finite and constant amount of energy in the universe, the first aspect of second law of thermodynamics states that the amount of usable energy in the universe grows smaller with each passing moment in time. The second aspect of the second law of thermodynamics is the law of entropy, which states if the universe and everything in it is left to itself over time, it will wear down, break down, and fall into disorder.

If we were to reverse time, we would find that there

would be a little more usable energy and a little more order in the universe; if we kept reversing time, we would reach a point in the past where the usable energy and order was at its maximum. The question becomes, how did the original energy and order get there? It is more reasonable to believe that someone put it there than to believe that the peak energy and order had no intelligent cause behind it coming into existence. We find the concept of the second law of thermodynamics right in the Old Testament, in Psalm 102:25-27:

"In the beginning you laid the foundations of the earth, and the heavens are the work of your hands. They will perish, but you remain; they will all wear out like a garment. Like clothing you will change them, and they will be discarded. But you remain the same, and your years will never end."

The thing you have to remember is that Psalm 102 was written around 900 B.C, and yet it accurately describes a scientific law that wasn't discovered by scientists until roughly 2,700 years later. How could the psalmist have possibly known that?

The second thing we'll look at is the expansion of the universe. In 1927, Edwin Hubble discovered red light shifts in every observable galaxy through his telescope, indicating to him that all the galaxies were moving away from each other. This is exactly what you would expect to see if the universe was expanding: If you were to watch the expansion of the universe in reverse, you would see the entire universe collapse back into nothing. In the beginning, there was nothing; then the entire physical universe came into existence.

We find this scientific fact recorded in the Old Testament. In Isaiah 40:22, 42:5, 44:24, 48:12-13, and 51:13, it is clearly stated that God is the one who stretches out the heavens. "Stretch" is a synonym for "expand", and anyone who studies the bible knows that the term "heavens" means "universe". How is it that the expansion of the universe was accurately described and mentioned 5 times in scriptures that were written between 740 and 680 BC when science didn't discover it until 1927?

The third thing I want to look at is the anthropic principle. There are over 120 anthropic constants in the universe that we've discovered so far, and if any single one of those constants were off in the slightest degree in any way, shape, or form, humanity would cease to exist. In other words, something is holding all these constants in place, keeping our universe and thus the human race alive. This makes absolute sense in light of Job 34:10-15:

"So listen to me, you men of understanding. Far be it from God to do evil, from the Almighty to do wrong. He repays everyone for what they have done; he brings on them what their conduct deserves. It is unthinkable that God would do wrong, that the Almighty would pervert justice. Who appointed him over the earth? Who put him in charge of the whole world? If it were his intention, and he withdrew his spirit and breath, all humanity would perish together and mankind would return to the dust."

In light of the anthropic principle, what Paul had to say about Jesus makes total sense:

Colossians 1:15-17: *"The Son is the image of the invisible God, the firstborn over all creation. For in him all things were created: things in heaven and on earth, visible and invisible, whether thrones or powers or rulers or authorities; all things have been created through him and for him. He is before all things, and in him all things hold together."*

The author of Hebrews makes a similar assertion in regards to Jesus and the anthropic principle:

Hebrews 1:1-4: *"In the past God spoke to our ancestors through the prophets at many times and in various ways, but in these last days he has spoken to us by his Son, whom he appointed heir of all things, and through whom also he made the universe. The Son is the radiance of God's glory and the exact representation of his being, sustaining all things by his powerful word. After he had provided purification for sins, he sat down at the right hand of the Majesty in heaven. So he became as much superior to the angels as the name he has inherited is superior to theirs."*

What should be creepy or eerie to every non-believer is that the second law of thermodynamics, the expansion of the universe, and the anthropic principle were accurately described thousands of years in advance of modern science by the same collection of scriptures called the Bible that teaches that the earth and universe are roughly 6,000 years old.

These evidences, as powerful as they are, do not specifically point towards the earth being 6,000 years old; you can find old earth creationists appealing to those same evidences to prove that their worldview is true. Let's get into two evidences that point strongly towards the earth being 6,000 years old.

THE DECAY RATE OF EARTH'S MAGNETIC FIELD

In a 2010 article titled "Earth's Magnetic Field", John D. Morris wrote the following about earth's magnetic field:

"Earth is surrounded by a powerful magnetic field, generated by well-understood and well-documented electric currents in its metallic core. Incoming solar and stellar radiation continually bombards earth and does great damage to life, causing harmful mutations and likely contributing to the aging and death of living things. Indeed, if these rays were not impeded and filtered by earth's magnetic field, life here would be impossible.

The strength of the magnetic field has been reliably and continually measured since 1835. From these measurements, we can see that the field's strength has declined by about seven percent since then, giving a half-life of about 1,400 years. This means that in 1,400 years it will be one-half as strong, in 2,800 years it will be one-fourth as strong, and so on. There will be a time not many thousands of years distant when the field will be too small to perform as a viable shield for earth.

Calculating back into the past, the present measurements indicate that 1,400 years ago the field was twice as strong. It continues doubling each 1,400 years back, until about 10,000 years ago it would have been so strong the planet would have disintegrated--its metallic core would have separated from its mantle. The inescapable conclusion *we can draw is that the earth must be fewer than 10,000 years old."* (5)

As we can see, the earth's magnetic field has been measured on a consistent basis since 1835, and based off what we've observed, we assume that the earth's magnetic field has a half-life of 1,400 years. If that assumption is true, then what this means is that 10,000 years ago, the earth's magnetic field would have been so powerful that it would have ripped the planet's core from the mantle, and earth would have disintegrated like Superman's home planet Krypton.

How can you have evolution occuring on earth over millions and billions of years when 10,000 years ago, there would not have been an earth to evolve on?

Of course, the evolutionists and atheists do not like the problem that the decay rate of the earth's magnetic field presents to their worldview's truthfulness, and so when young earth creationists present this problem to them, the evolutionists and atheists already have a response all lined up.

Back in 1995, Lenny Flank wrote an article titled "Creationists And 'Magnetic Field Decay'". It is in this article that Flank wrote the following:

"The Barnes/Humphreys hypothesis does not stand up to analysis. Barnes is correct that the dipole element of the magnetic field has indeed decreased in strength since the 19th century. However, as geologist Brent Dalrymple points out, "Barnes completely neglects the nondipole field. The same observatory measurements that show that the dipole moment has decreased since the early 1800's also show that this decrease has almost been completely balanced by an increase in the strength of the total observed field which has remained almost constant." (6)

As we can see, the evolutionist response to the problem of the decay rate of the earth's magnetic field is to say that while the dipole element of the magnetic field has been decaying at the rate that creationists like Morris outlined, what creationists like Morris neglect is that the nondipole element of the earth's magnetic field has increased since 1835, and as a result, the total observed magnetic field has remained almost constant.

This sounds like a winning counter-argument by the evolutionists until you continue to examine their writings regarding the problem of the decay rate of the Earth's magnetic field.

In 1998, *Scientific American* put out an article by Richard Brill titled "Is it true that the strength of the Earth's magnetic field is decreasing? What's the effect?". It is in this article that Brill writes the following:

"At most places there has been a general decrease in the strength over the past century, typically ten percent or so. No one can say with any certainty whether this represents a fluctuation or whether it is a decrease which will eventually lead to a reversal. Past reversals have taken place over a short period of time geologically speaking, 10,000 years or so. In order for a reversal to take place there must be a brief time during which the field is non existent." (7)

So according to evolutionists, the last magentic field reversal for the earth occured at least 10,000 years ago, and when that magnetic field reversal occured, there was a period of time where there was no magnetic field.

What would the consequences be for the Earth if there was no magnetic field around it?

Back in February of 2015, Johnathan Fuentes wrote an aritcle for the publication *Futurism* titled "6 Horrible Consequences of Earth Losing its Magnetic Field". It is in this article, Fuentes wrote the following:

"Our magnetic field doesn't just give us beautiful auroras: it keeps us alive. Cosmic rays and the solar wind are harmful to life on Earth, and without the protection of our magnetosphere, our planet would be constantly bombarded by a stream of deadly particles. The effects of cosmic rays on the body can be pretty terrifying. While on lunar missions, for example, astronauts often reported seeing flashes of light when they closed their eyes – the direct result of cosmic rays passing through their retinas. A few even developed cataracts years later.

Radiation and cosmic rays are a real concern for NASA, especially when it comes to long-term spaceflight. Astronauts on a mission to Mars could undergo up to 1000 times the exposure to radiation and cosmic rays that they would get on Earth. If Earth's magnetic field disappeared, the entire human race – and all of life, in fact – would be in serious danger. Cosmic rays would bombard our bodies and could even damage our DNA, increasing worldwide risk of cancer and other illnesses. The flashes of light visible when we close our eyes would be the least of our problems." (8)

According to Fuentes and *Futurism* (both are non-christian and non-creationist to my knowledge), if the Earth's magnetic field were to dissappear for a period of time like

Scientific American says it did 10,000 years ago, then all life on earth would be in serious danger because our bodies would be bombarded by cosmic rays, and all life on earth would ultimately be wiped out.

What is the point of all this?

When creationists like John D. Morris point out that 10,000 years ago the earth's magnetic field would have been so strong that the earth would have disintegrated, which is a problem that doesn't exist if the earth and universe are 6,000 years old like the Bible says, the evolutionists in response will say that the total observed magnetic field has been almost constant since we started measuring in 1835, and therefore the creationist is presenting a false dilema.

However, when you actually examine the writings of the evolutionists regarding earth's magnetic field, they acknowledge that 10,000 years ago, the earth's magnetic field would not have existed for a period of time, and they acknowledge that all life on earth would be wiped out by cosmic rays from space if there was no magnetic field around the earth. Human beings wouldn't be around to talk about it today if what the writings of evolutionists say are true regarding earth's magnetic field.

I actually agree with the evolutionists that there would not have been a magnetic field around the earth 10,000 years ago. The reason I agree with them is because the earth and universe are only 6,131 years old according to the Bible, and so the magnetic field problem that evolutionists have to deal with does not exist in the biblical worldview.

SOFT TISSUE INSIDE DINOSAUR BONES

The second piece of evidence that points towards young earth creationism being true is the existence of soft tissue inside of non-fossilized triceratops bone. But in order to understand the full impact of that discoverey, some background information is required.

In a 2006, *Discover* magazine put out an article titled "Schwietzer's Dangerous Discovery" documenting Mary Schwietzer's discovery of soft tissue inside a T-rex fossil. It is in this article that we read the following:

"Ever since Mary Higby Schweitzer peeked inside the fractured thighbone of a Tyrannosaurus rex, the introverted scientist's life hasn't been the same. Neither has the field of paleontology. Two years ago, Schweitzer gazed through a microscope in her laboratory at North Carolina State University and saw lifelike tissue that had no business

inhabiting a fossilized dinosaur skeleton: fibrous matrix, stretchy like a wet scab on human skin; what appeared to be supple bone cells, their three-dimensional shapes intact; and translucent blood vessels that looked as if they could have come straight from an ostrich at the zoo." (9)

The evolution paradigm says that dinosaurs died out a minimum of 65 million years ago. If that is true, then there shouldn't be soft tissue of any kind in any dinosaur fossil because there is no mechanism that allows soft tissue to be preserved for millions of years. And yet, Mary Schwietzer discovered soft tissue inside of a T-rex fossil.

The evolutionist community was in a panic because they knew their paradigm of history didn't allow for things like soft tissue inside of dinosaur fossils to exist, but they didn't want people to look to alternatives like young earth creationism to account for the existence of soft tissue inside of dinosaur fossils, and so they had to come up with a naturalistic explanation that allowed soft tissue to be preseverved inside dinosaur fossils over millions of years.

That's where Mary Schwietzer came in yet again.

In November of 2013, North Carolina State University put out an article on their news site titled "Iron Preserves, Hides Ancient Tissues in Fossilized Remains". It is in this article that we read the following:

"Mary Schweitzer, an NC State paleontologist with a
joint appointment at the N. C. Museum of Natural Sciences,
first announced the surprising preservation of soft tissues in
a T. rex fossil in 2005. Her subsequent work identified
proteins in the soft tissue that seemed to confirm that the
tissue was indeed T. rex tissue that had been preserved for
millions of years. But the findings remained controversial in
part because no one understood the chemical processes
behind such preservation.

Schweitzer's latest research shows that the presence of
hemoglobin – the iron-containing molecule that transports
oxygen in red blood cells – may be the key to both preserving
and concealing original ancient proteins within fossils. Her
results appear in Proceedings of the Royal Society B.

'Iron is necessary for survival, but it's also highly
reactive and destructive in living tissues, which is why our
bodies have proteins that transport iron molecules to where
they are needed but protect us from unwanted reactions at
the same time,' Schweitzer says. 'When we die, that protective
mechanism breaks down and the iron is turned loose on our
tissues – and that destructive process can act in much the
same way formaldehyde does to preserve the tissues and

47

proteins.'"

As we can see, Mary Schweitzer is claiming that iron acts as a preservative, and that this is how soft tissue can be preserved over millions of years inside of a fossil. What experiment did Schweitzer perform that supposedly proves her claim? Schweitzer goes on to explain that experiment:

"Schweitzer and her team noticed that iron particles are intimately associated with the soft tissues preserved in dinosaurs. But when they chelated – or removed the iron from – soft tissues taken from a T. rex and a Brachyolophosaurus, the chelated tissues reacted much more strongly to antibodies that detect the presence of protein, suggesting that the iron may be masking their presence in these preserved tissues. They then tested the preservation hypothesis by using blood vessels and cells taken from modern ostrich bone. They soaked some of these vessels in hemoglobin taken from red blood cells, while placing other vessels in water. Two years later, the hemoglobin-treated soft vessels remained intact, while those soaked in water degraded in less than a week." (10)

So what Mary Schweitzer and her team did was take the blood vessels and cells from ostrich bones, and covered some of them with iron in the form of hemoglobin, while placing others in water. They then left these blood vessels and cells in lab storage for two years, and when they revisited these blood vessels and cells, they found that the ones covered in iron were still intact, while those soaked in water degraded in less than a week.

The entire atheist, evolutionist, and leftist establishment praised Schweitzer when NCU put out their press release, and they claimed that Schweitzer had proven how soft tissue can survive inside of dinosaur fossils over millions of years. Little did they know that God was 10 steps ahead of them, and allowed young earth creationist Mark Armitage to discover something that would upset the new establishment narrative of iron preserving soft tissue over millions of years.

On May 12, 2012 on a private ranch in the Hell Creek Formation near Jordan, Montana, Mark Armitage and his team were able to excavate an unusal dinosar bone. Armitage explained his discovery in his "Soft sheets of fibrillar bone from a fossil of the supraorbital horn of the dinosaur Triceratops horridus" paper:

"An intact Triceratops horn (HCTH-00) was recovered on May 12, 2012, from a well-sorted fluvial sandstone within the Hell Creek Formation at a previously unexcavated site on

a private ranch within the Hell Creek Formation (a portion of land located at E 1/2 of the SW 1/4 of the NE 1/4 Section 14, T. 15 N., R. 56 E., Dawson County, Glendive, MT, USA). The recovered horn was jacketed and removed. The length, girth and external morphology of the fossil was consistent with other Triceratops horns recovered from the Hell Creek Formation. Disarticulated Triceratops ribs (HCTR-11) and vertebrae (HCTV-22) found within a mile of the horn were also recovered for analysis.

Hand-sized pieces of HCTH-00 were fixed in 2.5% glutaraldehyde solution, buffered with 0.1 M sodium cacodylate buffer at 4 °C for 5 days, rinsed in distilled water and buffer and stored in phosphate buffered saline (PBS). Individual pieces of roughly 20 cm2 were removed by pressure fracture (HCTH-01, 02, 03), examined under a dissecting microscope and probed with sterile forceps to identify and collect soft material. Soft materials recovered were washed in double distilled water and stored in PBS awaiting further analysis.

Other horn specimens (HCTH-04, 05) were processed through a decalcification protocol. Several pieces about 20–50 cm in size were rinsed in double distilled water after fixation and were incubated in a solution of 14% sodium

EDTA at room temperature. EDTA was exchanged every 2–4 days for a period of 4 weeks. Significant bone mineral remained after 4 weeks,therefore it was unknown whether complete decalcification would yield soft and transparent, vessellike tissues such as previously reported." (11)

As we can see from the paper, what Mark Armitage discovered in the Hell Creek Formation in 2012 was a triceratops horn. Armitage was able to use pressure fracture to split up the horn into five different pieces. Two of the pieces were fossilized, and so Armitage had to process those pieces through the decalcification process. The other three pieces, however, were not fossilized, and so all Armitage did with those pieces was wash them in distilled water and store them. In the three pieces that were not fossilized, Armitage discovered soft tissue inside of them.

This was a world-shattering discovery because Mary Schwietzer's theory about iron preserving soft tissues over millions of years was only an explanation of how soft tissue could survive inside of a fossilized dinosaur bone over millions of years. Armitage's discovery of soft tissue inside non-fossilized dinosaur bone that he found just under the surface of the harsh climate of the Hell Creek Formation cannot be explained by Schweitzer's theory because according to the atheist evolutionist paradigm of history, it is impossible for soft tissue to survive for millions of years inside of non-fossilized dinosaur bone, especially when that bone is just under the surface of a place like the Hell Creek Formation.

When discussing his discovery in his YouTube videos, Mark Armitage has talked about how his discovery shows that humans and dinosaurs walked the earth at the same time in the past, a conclusion that you come to if you accept the young earth creationism timeline of history that the Bible teaches.

What was Mark Armitage's reward for his amazing discovery?

Shortly after he published his paper about his discovery, an official at Cal State University Northridge (the university Armitage worked at) went to Armitage's office and told him, "We are not going to tolerate your religion in this department!" Not too long after that, Armitage was fired from CSUN. (12) Armitage then filed a lawsuit against CSUN for wrongful termination, and after two years, CSUN settled out of court with Armitage. (13)

FULLY-DEVELOPED ORGANISMS APPEAR IN THE FOSSIL RECORD

Evolutionists and atheists today claim that the fossil record is one of the strongest evidences supporting the atheistic evolutionary worldview, but as you are about to see, the fossil record is actually one of the strongest evidences for young earth creationism in the world of science.

In his 1983 book *Science On Trial: The Case For Evolution*, evolutionist Douglas Futuyma wrote the following:

"Creation and evolution, between them, exhaust the possible explanations for the origin of living things. Organisms either appeared on the earth fully developed or they did not. If they did not, they must have developed from preexisting species by some process of modification. If they did appear in a fully developed state, they must have been created by some omnipotent intelligence." (14)

As you can see, Futuyma says that if organisms appear in the fossil record in a fully developed state, this is definitive proof that those organisms were created by an all-powerful intelligent mind. In other words, if organisms appear in the fossil record in a fully developed state with no evolutionary history behind them, this is irrefutable evidence that they were designed by the God of the Bible, and this also would be scientific evidence for young earth creationism.

The question at this point is, do we find organisms in a fully developed state in the fossil record?

Paleontologists tell us that during the period of time in the fossil record that they call the Cambrian Explosion, all the major animal forms and groups appeared all at once out of nothing in an instant, without a single trace of less complex ancestors. This led the evolutionist Richard Dawkins to write the following in his 1986 book *The Blind Watchmaker*:

"And we find many of them already in an advanced state of evolution, the very first time they appear. It is as though they were just planted there, without any evolutionary history. Needless to say, this appearance of sudden planting has delighted creationists..." (15)

So according to Dawkins, when we look at the fossil record, we see that many, if not all, of the organisms in it were in a fully developed state from the moment they entered the fossil record, and that this discovery has delighted creationists like myself. Young earth creationists like myself are indeed delighted by this discovery because evolutionists like Futuyma said that this is what we would find in the fossil record if young earth creationism is true. Since this is what we find in the fossil record, this means that we have scientific evidence supporting young earth creationism.

Of course, evolutionists and atheists to this day ignore this and continue to assert that there is no scientific evidence supporting young earth creationism, and they try to get young earth creationism black-balled from society so that nobody knows about young earth creationism and the evidence supporting it, but we'll get into that more in chapter two.

NEGATIVE FEELINGS THAT COME FROM BEING LIED TO ABOUT ORIGINS

If you're a young earth creationist reading this book, and if you started out as an old earth creationist before converting to young earth creationism like I did, then you may have experienced anger when you first found out that old earth creationism was false and young earth creationism was true. You may have felt like you had been lied to by your church leaders as well as the secular world. I know that I did, and fellow young earth creationist JD Mitchell expressed similar sentiment when he wrote the following in the prologue of his book *The Creation Dialogues*:

> *"I cannot blame the university for all of this because I got no help on the subject of origins from my church back home, and I was personally very open to the concepts of evolution as presented in my high school biology, chemistry, and physics classes. At my high school, the tradition held that each year we'd sign the yearbooks of friends and acquaintances and add pithy comments for posterity. I was honored that my chemistry teacher signed his name and next to his comment he wrote 'Big Bang or Steady State—that is the question.' I took this to mean he felt I held sufficient promise to be able to decide the correct theory for the natural condition of the universe once I completed my education.*
>
> *Nevertheless in 1984, some 17 years after I graduated from college, I was very angry. I don't know if I was angrier at the church or at the secular educators, but I do know that I felt I had been lied to for decades regarding origins truth."* (16)

Feeling angry about the fact that you were lied to about the truth regarding origins is a natural reaction, but one thing you have to keep in mind is that not everyone who lied to you about origins did so intentionally. While some of the people who lied to us about origins and the age of the earth and universe know that the Bible completely contradicts what they tell, some of the people who lied to us have no idea that the Bible teaches something completely different from what they've been told throughout their educational experience, which is that big bang cosmology, billions of years, and evolution are true. Discerning which one is which can be very difficult to do, but we must go easier on those who unintentionally lied to us about origins.

YOUNG EARTH CREATIONISM IS A SALVATION ISSUE

To wrap things up in this chapter, we must discuss something that is so controversial that not only do atheists, evolutionists, and old earth creationists reject it, but even most people who identify as young earth creationists refuse to accept it.

Young Earth Creationism is a salvation issue.

As we saw at the beginning of this chapter, we saw the Bible clearly teach through Exodus 20:8-11 and Exodus 31:12-

17 that the days of creation were ordinary days like we experience today. We also saw towards the beginning of this chapter that the Bible provides the genealogies and time spans that cover the entire time between the beginning of the earth and universe all the way up to the fourth year of King Solomon's reign, which leads you to the conclusion that the Earth and universe are 6,131 years old when you look at the time that has passed since the fourth year of King Solomon's reign.

How can we know for sure that the straight forward reading of those passages is true, and how does this make young earth creationism a salvation issue?

It's really quite simple.

In Numbers 12, we read about the account of when Miriam and Aaron opposed Moses and challenged his authority as the prophet from God. After God summoned them all to the tent of meeting, God said the following to Miriam and Aaron:

Numbers 12:6-9: *"he said, 'Listen to my words:*

When there is a prophet among you, I, the Lord, reveal

myself to them in visions, I speak to them in dreams. But this is not true of my servant Moses; he is faithful in all my house. With him I speak face to face, clearly and not in riddles; he sees the form of the Lord. Why then were you not afraid to speak against my servant Moses?'

The anger of the Lord burned against them, and he left them."

God makes it clear in this passage that when he revealed his revelations to Moses, he did not speak to Moses in a dream or vision. This is important because there are Christians who actually believe and teach that God revealed his revelations to Moses through dreams and/or visions. God himself flat out says that such was not the case with Moses, and that he actually spoke to Moses face to face.

God also says in this passage that He spoke to Moses clearly, and not in riddles. When he said this, God made it painfully clear that he not only spoke to Moses in a straight-forward manner, but he also made it clear that he did not speak to Moses in any kind of coded language. This part directly condemns old earth creationists because old earth creationists teach that God spoke to Moses in some kind of coded language that leads you to believe in deep time and old earth creationism when deciphered properly.

Since God clearly said in Numbers 12:6-9 that he spoke to Moses in a straight-forward manner when he revealed his revelations to Moses, this means that the only correct interpretation of what Moses wrote in the Torah is the straight-forward, contextual reading of what Moses wrote.

Since the straight-forward reading of what Moses wrote leads you to the conclusion that the Bible teaches that the earth and universe are a little over 6,000 years old, this means that anything contradicts it is a heresy if it comes from the lips of someone who claims to be a follower of Jesus.

There are some who would respond to this by saying that even though the Bible clearly teaches a 6,000 year old earth and universe, young earth creationism cannot be a salvation issue because the age of the earth is never specifically mentioned in any Bible passages that tell us how to get saved. Such a response is quite silly if you think about it.

The Bible clearly makes many different historical claims that most Christians would not deny. For example, the gospels say that Jesus healed the sick. The gospels also say that Jesus was born of a virgin, and that he drove out demons. Jesus also claimed to be Yahweh in John 8:58. According to Deuteronomy 29:5, God prevented the clothes and sandals of the Israelites from wearing out while they were wandering the desert for 40 years. According to both Exodus 3 and Jesus, God spoke to Moses in the form of a burning bush.

Most Christians who reject the idea of young earth creationism being a salvation issue would tell you that if you claim to be a Christian but reject any of the above claims that the Bible makes, you would clearly be a heretic who is not saved. None of the things listed in the previous paragraph are listed as requirements for salvation in any of the Bible passages that deal with salvation, but most Christians rightly understand that to reject things that the Bible clearly teaches is a rejection of biblical inerrancy. Most Christians also understand that biblical inerrancy is a salvation issue.

Following that logic, because the Bible clearly teaches a 6,000 year old earth and universe, and because rejecting things that the Bible clearly teaches is a rejection of biblical inerrancy, and because biblical inerrancy is a salvation issue, this means that young earth creationism is a salvation issue.

When I point out that young earth creationism is a salvation issue, there are many who have responded to me by saying, "but I know Christians who accepted the gospel message of salvation, and they've never heard of young earth creationism before. Are you saying that those kind of christians are not saved?"

People who hear me say that young earth creationism is a salvation issue get the impression that I'm teaching that Christians who have never heard of young earth creationism are not saved, and so they are usually surprised or relieved when I explain to them that those kinds of Christians can still be saved people.

In the gospel of Luke, we find a teaching of Jesus that is relevant to this topic:

Luke 12:47-48: *"The servant who knows the master's will and does not get ready or does not do what the master wants will be beaten with many blows. But the one who does not know and does things deserving punishment will be beaten with few blows. From everyone who has been given much, much will be demanded; and from the one who has been entrusted with much, much more will be asked."*

In this passage, we can see Jesus teaching that God holds people accountable for what they know, and that God does not hold people accountable for things they do not know.

How this applies to the issue of young earth creationism and salvation is simple: If you had the gospel message of salvation preached to you, but you were never exposed to the Bible's teaching of a 6,000 year-old earth and universe, then God is going to judge you based on whether or not you accepted the gospel message of salvation, and he will not judge you for whether or not you accept the teaching of young earth creationism that you were never exposed to.

Inversly, if you exposed to the 6,000 year-old earth and universe that the Bible teaches, and it's explained to you exactly how the Bible teacehs that, and you reject it while simultaneously claiming to be a Bible believer and Jesus follower, then God will hold you accountable for rejecting what he said about origins, and you will have proven that you are not saved because saved Bible belivers do not reject any of the clear teachings of the Bible. As Jesus said:

Matthew 7:15-20: *"Watch out for false prophets. They come to you in sheep's clothing, but inwardly they are ferocious wolves. By their fruit you will recognize them. Do people pick grapes from thornbushes, or figs from thistles? Likewise, every good tree bears good fruit, but a bad tree bears bad fruit. A good tree cannot bear bad fruit, and a bad tree cannot bear good fruit. Every tree that does not bear good fruit is cut down and thrown into the fire. Thus, by their fruit you will recognize them."*

Jesus clearly taught that we will recognize whether someone is a true believer or not by the fruits they bear. For example, if someone is a true Bible believer, they will accept every clear teaching that comes from a straight-forward and contextual reading of the Bible. But if someone claims to be a Bible-believer while simultaneously rejecting any of the clear teachings that come from a straight-forward reading of the Bible, then they prove that they are not really a Bible believer.

Now that we have gone through the biblical evidence for young earth creationism as well as observable evidence in reality that supports it, we are going to transition to talking about atheistic evolution in the next chapter.

Chapter 2

Atheistic Evolution

A RELIGION DISGUISED AS SCIENCE

When it comes to the issue of origins, there is much opposition to young earth creationism's 6,000 year timeline of history. The two main groups of people who oppose young earth creationism are old earth creationists, and atheistic evolutionists.

There are Christians who believe in evolution, deep time, and big bang cosmology, but we will discuss them in chapter three when we discuss old earth creationism in more detail. In this chapter, we will be discussing the evolutionists who are atheists and agnostics, also known as atheistic evolutionists.

Atheistic evolutionists tell the world that evolution and deep time is science, and that young earth creationism is religion. They then say that because young earth creationism is religion, young earth creationism is not science. When pressed to explain why young earth creationism is not science, atheistic evolutionists will say that young earth creationism is not science because young earth creationism cannot be proven with observational science.

According to atheistic evolutionists, young earth creationism cannot be scientific because it relies on the Bible, which is based on God, and in accordance with their own definition of science, scientific explanations must always be materialistic. This is clearly a philosophical position.

What most atheistic evolutionists don't realize is that evolution and deep time cannot be proven with observational science, and they fail to realize that evolution and deep time is the very kind of religion that they claim to be against.

When they are told this by young earth creationists, atheistic evolutionists think and claim that the idea of evolution not being based on observational science is nothing more than false propaganda put out by young earth creationists. The reality is that this idea comes from one of the most die-hard evolutionists on planet earth, the late Ernst Mayr.

In a 2009 article "Darwin's Influence On Modern

Thought", evolutionist Ernst Mayr said the following:

"These four insights served as the foundation for Darwin's founding of a new branch of the philosophy of science, a philosophy of biology. Despite the passing of a century before this new branch of philosophy fully developed, its eventual form is based on Darwinian concepts. For example, Darwin introduced historicity into science. Evolutionary biology, in contrast with physics and chemistry, is a historical science—the evolutionist attempts to explain events and processes that have already taken place. Laws and experiments are inappropriate techniques for the explication of such events and processes. Instead one constructs a historical narrative, consisting of a tentative reconstruction of the particular scenario that led to the events one is trying to explain." (17)

As we can see, Ernst Mayr, one of the most die-hard evolutionists ever, admits that evolution is a historical science, and that it is inappropriate to use observational science to try and prove the claims found in the evolutionary paradigm of history. Mayr admits that evolution is a worldview through which one interprets reality.

There are some atheistic evolutionists who will probably be skeptical of my claim that Ersnt Mayr was a diehard evolutionist; some might even claim that the fact that mayr admitted that evolution is a worldview proves that Mayr is not a staunch evolutionist.

In an interview on a website called *Edge*, Mayr was asked by the interviewer if evolution was a fact or not. The following was Mayr's entire response:

"That's a very good question. Because of the historically entrenched resistance to the thought of evolution, documented by modern-day creationism, evolutionists have been forced into defending evolution and trying to prove that it is a fact and not a theory. Certainly the explanation of evolution and the search for its underlying ideas has been somewhat neglected, and my new book, the title of which is What Evolution Is, *is precisely attempting to rectify that situation. It attempts to explain evolution. As I say in the first section of the book, I don't need to prove it again, evolution is so clearly a fact that you need to be committed to something like a belief in the supernatural if you are at all in disagreement with evolution. It is a fact and we don't need to prove it anymore. Nonetheless we must explain why it happened and how it happens."* (18)

As we can see from this interview, Ernst Mayr claimed that evolution is such an established fact that we don't need to prove its truthfulness anymore. And yet, Ernst Mayr not only admits that evolution is not based on observational science, but he admits that it is inappropriate to try to use observational science to prove the truthfulness of evolution and deep time.

An atheistic evolutionist reading this may think to themselves, "how can an evolutionist like Mayr claim that evolution is such an established fact that we don't need to prove its truthfulness anymore while at the same time saying that it is inappropriate to use observational science to try and prove evolution?"

It's simple, really. The truth is that evolution and deep time is a religious worldview through which its adherents interpret all of reality through its lense. Even though evolution and deep time is a worldview that cannot be proven true through observational science, Mayr believes that the evolutionary worldview explains the facts of reality so much better than every other worldview that he believes that we don't need to prove the truthfulness of the evolutionary worldview anymore.

Now that we understand that evolution and deep time is a religious worldview, let us examine the evolutionary paradigm of history that atheists and evolutionists want us to accept as being true.

THE EVOLUTION PARADIGM OF HISTORY

The evolution paradigm teaches that according to the big bang theory, the universe came into existence 13.8 billion years ago. It also teaches that 4.567 billion years ago, the sun came into existence via a gravitational collapse of matter within a molecular cloud. This theory also teaches that 4.54 billion years ago, the earth came into existence. Over the course of these billions of years, life not only came into existence from non-living material, but it also went from simple to more complex via natural selection and random chance mutations creating new genetic information that did not previously exist.

According to the evolution paradigm of history, microevolution is changes that occur within a family, and that microevolution over billions of years leads to macroevolution, which is when one family changes into another family. Not only are modern humans the end result of evolution from an ape-like ancestor over the course of six million years, but evolution teaches that all organic life has a single, universal common ancestor. All of this happened without any intelligent intervention from any kind of god, intelligent designer or intelligent mind of any kind.

This short summary of the evolution paradigm of history is sure to cause evolutionists to go into a violent rage because they don't like seeing their worldview summarized in a way that most people can understand. Some evolutionists will probably even claim that the evolution paradigm of history doesn't teach all of the things I listed. For those evolutionists, let's show them evidence that the evolution paradigm of history really does teach all the things that I said it does.

If you go to the Wikipedia or InfoGalactic entries for the universe, you will find that they say that the universe came into existence 13.8 billion years ago via the big bang theory. Since the Wikipedia and InfoGalactic entries contain the current consensus of the scientific and academic community regarding the age of the universe as well as how it came into existence, I doubt that evolutionists will disagree with me pointing out that the evolution paradigm of history teaches that the universe came into existence 13.8 billion years ago via big bang theory.

We have a similar situation with the age of the earth and sun. If you go to the Wikipedia entries for the sun and the earth, they say that the sun came into existence 4.6 billion years ago, and that the earth came into existence 4.5 billion years ago. The InfoGalactic entries say that the sun came into existence via a gravitational collapse of matter within a molecular cloud 4.567 billion years ago, and that the earth came into existence 4.54 billion years ago. Both the Wikipedia entries and the InfoGalactic entries for the sun and earth clearly teach that the sun came into existence before the earth. I don't see any sane evolutionist denying that the evolution paradigm of history teaches these things.

While no evolutionist would disagree with me that life came into existence from non-living material, how do we know that the evolution paradigm of history teaches that life went from simple to more complex via natural selection and mutations? How do we know that microevolution is changes that occur within a family, and that microevolution over billions of years leads to macroevolution, which is when one family changes into another family?

In the article "Introduction: Evolution" on *NewScientist*, we read the following:

"Evolution has several facets. The first is the theory that all living species are the modified descendents of earlier species, and that we all share a common ancestor in the distant past. All species are therefore related via a vast tree of life. The second is that this evolution is driven by a process of natural selection or the – "survival of the fittest". (19)

This article from *NewScientist* makes it clear that the

evolution paradigm of history teaches that life went from simple to more complex over billions of years via natural selection.

When it comes to microevolution and macroevolution, let's turn our attention to an evolutionist website called *Understanding Evolution.* This website is a collaborative project between the University of California Museum of Paleontology and the National Center for Science Education. The NCSE is considered an authoritative source of information within the evolutionist camp, so they can be trusted to tell us the truth about what the evolution worldview paradigm teaches regarding microevolution and macroevolution.

In an article on the *Understanding Evolution* website called "What Is Microevolution?", we read the following:

"Microevolution is simply a change in gene frequency within a population. Evolution at this scale can be observed over short periods of time — for example, between one generation and the next, the frequency of a gene for pesticide resistance in a population of crop pests increases. Such a change might come about because natural selection favored the gene, because the population received new immigrants carrying the gene, because some nonresistant genes mutated to the resistant version, or because of random genetic drift

from one generation to the next." (20)

As we can see from this article, the evolution paradigm teaches that microevolution is changes that occur within a species via natural selection and mutations.

In the article called "What is Macroevolution?", we read the following:

"Macroevolution generally refers to evolution above the species level. So instead of focusing on an individual beetle species, a macroevolutionary lens might require that we zoom out on the tree of life, to assess the diversity of the entire beetle clade and its position on the tree."

Later on in the article, we read this:

"A process like mutation might seem too small-scale to influence a pattern as amazing as the beetle radiation, or as large as the difference between dogs and pine trees, but it's not. Life on Earth has been accumulating mutations and passing them through the filter of natural selection for 3.8 billion years — more than enough time for evolutionary processes to produce its grand history." (21)

As we can see from this article, the evolution paradigm of history teaches that macroevolution is when one family changes into another, and this supposedly happens when microevolution goes on over billions of years.

When you read the article "Introduction To Human Evolution" on the *Smithsonian National Museum of Natural History* website, you see the following:

"Human evolution is the lengthy process of change by which people originated from apelike ancestors. Scientific evidence shows that the physical and behavioral traits shared by all people originated from apelike ancestors and evolved over a period of approximately six million years." (22)

In other words, the evolution paradigm of history teaches that human beings are the end result of six million years of evolution from an ape-like ancestor.

When you point out that the evolution paradigm of history teaches that all organic life has a single, universal common ancestor, evolutionists will vehemently deny it. They'll claim that evolution doesn't specifically teach that. Don't take my word for it though.

On July 7, 2018, an evolutionist YouTuber named Professor Stick put out a video titled "Antibiotic Resistance Is Apparently Not Evolution", a video that has over 69,000 views. In this video, Professor Stick was attempting to refute a creationist YouTuber called iApologia. At one point in the video, iApologia said that evolution teaches that all organic life has a single, universal common ancestor. It is in this video where Professor Stick said the following in response to iApologia:

"So you don't know the actual definition of Darwinian evolution. See, while those conclusions can be drawn by scientists working in the field of evolution, Darwinian evolution doesn't actually directly state that." (23)

Unfortunately for evolutionists like Professor Stick, the claim that the evolution paradigm of history teaches that all organic life descended from a single, universal common ancestor is not the invention of creationists like myself or iApologia. This claim comes directly from Charles Darwin.

On page 484 of Darwin's *On The Origin Of Species By Means Of Natural Selection, Or The Preservation Of Favoured Races In The Struggle For Life*, we find Charles Darwin saying the following:

"I believe that animals have descended from at most only four or five progenitors, and plants from an equal or lesser number.

Analogy would lead me one step further, namely, to

the belief that all animals and plants have descended from some one prototype. But analogy may be a deceitful guide. Nevertheless all living things have much in common, in their chemical composition, their germinal vesicles, their cellular structure, and their laws of growth and reproduction. We see this even in so trifling a circumstance as that the same poison often similarly affects plants and animals; or that the poison secreted by the gall-fly produces monstrous growths on the wild rose or oak-tree. Therefore I should infer from analogy that probably all the organic beings which have ever lived on this earth have descended from some one primordial form, into which life was first breathed." (24)

Charles Darwin is the founder of darwinian evolution, so it stands to reason that if Darwin teaches something about evolution, then darwinian evolution teaches it. As we can clearly see from Darwin's own writings, Darwin clearly taught that all organic life descended from a single, universal common ancestor. Therefore, the evolution paradigm of history teaches that all organic life descends from a single, universal common ancestor.

It is funny to see evolutionists deny that evolution teaches that all organic life descends from a single, universal common ancestor even though Charles Darwin himself taught the idea, but on the other hand, I don't blame them for reject a teaching of Darwin's that so blatantly contradicts all observation, intuition, and common sense.

Let's go into the fatal flaws with the evolution paradigm of history that prevent me from ever considering evolution as a serious worldview to hold.

THERE IS NO EVIDENCE FOR

BILLIONS OF YEARS

The first problem I have with evolution that is a fatal flaw is the concept that the earth and universe are billions of years old, which is also known as deep time. The concept of deep time was specifically designed not only to hide the non-existent evidence for evolution in a distant, unobservable past, but it was also designed to get people to reject the 6,000-year-old earth and universe that the Bible teaches. If people had not bought into the concept of deep time, then evolution and big bang cosmology would never have taken off, and would have died back in the 19th century.

Who came up with the concept of deep time? On page one of their book *James Hutton: The Founder Of Modern*

Geology, historical authors Donald McIntyre and Alan McKirdy wrote the following:

"Scientists currently think that the earth is four and a half billion years old. Our present knowledge is the culmination of two centuries of research, started by James Hutton, an Edinburgh man, who demonstrated that the earth was immensely old." (25)

Since James Hutton is credited as being the founder of the concept of deep time, one must ask what kind of observational evidence Hutton based his hypothesis on.

The strongest evidence that Hutton had supporting his concept of deep time was the unconformity of the geology at Siccar Point, a headland sticking out over the North Sea roughly 30 miles east of Edinburgh. In 1788, Hutton took John Playfair and Sir James Hall to Siccar Point, and the following account of what transpired there was given by Playfair and Hall:

"Dr. Hutton wished particularly to examine the latter of these [Siccar Point], and on this ocassion Sir James Hall and I had the pleasure to accompany him. We sailed in a boat from Dunglass, on a day when the fitness of the weather

permitted us to keep close to the foot of the rocks which line the shore in that quarter, directing our course southwards, in search of the termination of the secondary strata. We made for a high rocky point or headland, the SICCAR, near which, from out observastions on shore, we knew that the object we were in search of was likely to be discovered. On landing at this point, we found that we actually trode on the primeval rock, which forms alternately the base and the summit of the present land. It is here a micaceous schistus, in beds nearly vertical, highly indurated [hard], and stretching from S.E. To N.W. The surface of this rock runs with a moderate ascent from the level of low-water, at which we landed, nearly to that of high-water, where the schistus has a thin covering of red horizontal sandstone laid over it; and this sandstone, at the distance of a few yards farther back, rises into a very high perpendicular cliff. Here, therefore, the immediate contact of the two rocks is not only visible, but is curiously dissected and laid open by the action of the waves. The rugged tops of the schistus are seen penetrating into the horizontal beds of sandstone, and the lowest of these last form a breccia containing fragments of schistus, some round and others angular, united by an arenaceous cement.

Dr. Hutton was highly pleased with appearances that set in so clear a light the different formations of the parts which compose the exterior crust of the earth, and where all the circumstances were combined that could render the observation satisfactory and precise. On those who saw these phenomena for the first time, the impression made will not easily be forgotten. The palpable evidence presented to us, of one of the most extraordinary and important facts in the natural history of the earth, gave a reality and substance to those theoretical speculations, which however probable, had never till now been directly authenticated by the testimony of the senses. We often said to ourselves, what clearer evidence could we have had of the different formation of these rocks, and of the long interval which sperated their formation, had we actually seen them emerging from the bosom of the deep? We felt ourselves necessarily carried back to the time when the schistus on which we stood was yet at the bottom of the sea, and when the sandstone before us was only beginning to be deposited, in the shape of sand or mud, from the waters of a superincumbent ocean. An epocha still more remote presented itself, when even the most ancient of these rocks, instead of standing upright in vertical beds, lay in horizontal planes at the bottom of the sea, and was not yet disturbed by that iummeasurable force which has burst asunder the solid pavement of the globe. Revolutions still more remote appeared in the distance of this extraordinary perspective. The mind seemed to grow giddy by looking so far into the abyss of time; and while we listened with earnestness and admiration to the philosopher who was now unfolding to us the order and series of these wonderful events, we became sensible how much farther reason may sometimes go than immagination can venture to follow." (26)

As we can see from the accounts of Playfair and Hall, James Hutton noted that there were two different sections of strata at Siccar Point that were probably not laid down at the same time, and Hutton arbitrarily concluded that there must have been an incredibly long period of time that passed between each strata layer being laid down.

Young earth creationist author Milt Marcy offered his anaylsis of Playfair and Hall's account on page 75 of his book *The Emperors Who Had No Clothes*:

"Might I suggest that Hutton's imagination is all we have in that statement? Reason was tossed out the window long before.

There seems little doubt that Hutton was correct in surmising that the two sections of strata were laid down at different times, but jumping to the conclusion that they had to be seperated by eons of time is an unwarrented assumption.

They could just as easily have been seperated by only a few hours or days if their formation waa achieved by a catastrophic process. Playfair's and Hall's willingness to accept the vast age pruposed by Hutton rests on nothing more than their naivety and Hutton's status as an Edinburgh elite. They were accepting his authority instead of letting the evidence speak for itself and coming to their own conclusions. The fact that Hutton did not even mention the reigning paradigm of a catastrophic world flood in his Theory Of The Earth *is suspicious at best and devious at worst.*" (27)

As Marcy explains so clearly, the reason why Playfair and Hall were so willing to accept Hutton's arbitrary declaration that long periods of time passed between the laying down of each layer of strata at Siccar Point is because they were gullible guys who did not know any better, and they were wooed by Hutton's status as a member of the societal elite of Edinburgh. They viewed Hutton as their high priest when it came to the issue of origins, and the reverantial tone of their account of their visit to Siccar Point with Hutton bears that out.

In the 1800s, there was a geologist named Charles Lyell who was a firm believer in Hutton's work and concept of deep time. In 1830, Lyell put out the first of three volumes of his work *Principles of Geology*, a work that along with Hutton's work greatly influenced Charles Darwin's evolution theory that Darwin laid out in his 1859 book *On the origin of species by means of natural selection, or the preservation of favoured races in the struggle for life.*

In an 1830 letter that he wrote to Poulett Scrope, Lyell wrote the following:

"P.S – I have been very careful in my work in referring, where I have borrowed, to authors, and am not conscious of ever having done so without citing in a note. I doubt whether I have embodied sentences from any author so much as from you, and you will see that that is in great moderation.

I concieved the idea five or six years ago, that if ever the Mosaic geology could be set down without giving offence, it would be in an historical sketch, and you must abstract mine, in order to have as little to say as possible yourself. Let them feel it, and point the moral." (28)

On page 105 of *The Emperors Who Had No Clothes*, Marcy offered the following analysis of Lyell's letter to Scrope:

"Scrope, Lyell's personal friend, was writing the review of his first book, Principles of Geology *for the* Quarterly Review, *and Lyell was giving him advice on what he wanted to see in the review!Sounds like neither objectivity nor honesty were his highest priority! Note especially the last paragraph. If we were to put that into modern English: 'In order to destory Genesis 1-11, and thereby all of the Bible, you must not attack it directly, but just give a factual account that contradicts it and say as little as possible yourself. When they think over the implications of what you've said they will see that the Bible is not a reliable document, but they will not blame you for that fact.' Never mind that many of the 'facts' in the 'factual account' are false. This was the whole modus operandi of Charles Lyell, given here in one paragraph. A very crafty man indeed!"* (29)

As Lyell's letter to Scrope proves, and Marcy's analysis confirms, the whole point of the concept of deep time and the earth & universe being billions of years old was to get people to reject the creation account of Genesis 1:1-2:3, the flood of Noah, and the genealogies and time spans provided by the Bible that lead you to the conclusion that the earth and universe are 6,000 years old. The way that Hutton and Lyell's deep time conept would do this is that it would present what seemed like a factual account that contradicts what the Bible

85

says.

In summary, the whole concept of the earth being billions of years old is not based on any observational evidence. It was literally founded on an arbitrary assumption that deep, long periods of time passed between each sediment layer on earth being laid down, and it was specifically designed to get people to reject the Bible's clear teaching that the earth and universe are only 6,000 years old.

EVOLUTION IS IMPOSSIBLE, EVEN IN PRINCIPLE

Another fatal flaw with the evolution paradigm of history is that not only does evolution take so long to occur that nobody can live long enough to see it happen in action, but there is a scientific law that actually makes it impossible for evolution to occur.

There are two facts about the evolution paradigm of history that are irrefutable. The first is that the evolution paradigm of history teaches that the process of evolution takes so long to occur that nobody can live long enough to see it happen in action. This was illustrated perfectly when Stephen Jay Gould said the following in his 1981 publication *Evolution*

As Fact And Theory:

"In 1972 my colleague Niles Eldredge and I developed the theory of punctuated equilibrium. We argued that two outstanding facts of the fossil record—geologically "sudden" origin of new species and failure to change thereafter (stasis) —reflect the predictions of evolutionary theory, not the imperfections of the fossil record. In most theories, small isolated populations are the source of new species, and the process of speciation takes thousands or tens of thousands of years. This amount of time, so long when measured against our lives, is a geological microsecond. It represents much less than 1 per cent of the average life-span for a fossil invertebrate species—more than ten million years. Large, widespread, and well established species, on the other hand, are not expected to change very much. We believe that the inertia of large populations explains the stasis of most fossil species over millions of years." (30)

The lack of evidence for evolution occurring in small, gradual changes over millions of years was so damning that Gould and his colleague Niles Eldridge came up with the punctuated equilibrium theory, which theorizes that evolution happened so fast that it left behind no evidence. But even in his punctuated equilibrium theory, Gould acknowledged that evolution takes so long to occur that nobody can live long enough to see it happen in action, which is why he said "This amount of time, so long when measured against our lives, is a geological milisecond".

The second irrefutable fact of the evolution paradigm is that all of the evolutionary history that we are told about in school occurred before human beings with the ability to make records of their observations ever came along.

Why do these two irrefutable facts about the evolution paradigm of history create a fatal flaw with the paradigm?

If nobody can live long enough to see evolution happen in action, then that means that nobody could record it as a historical event. This also means that nobody can set up an experiment to verify or falsify that evolution in the macro sense is a naturally-occurring phenomenon. This logically means that evolution is not, and can never be, considered science, or be considered a fact of science.

The only way that anyone can believe that evolution, billions of years, and big bang cosmology is true is that they have to believe that the authority figure or group of authority figures telling them that evolution, deep time, and big bang cosmology is true are telling them the truth, and that such people are incapable of leading them astray in regards to origins.

On top of the fact that evolution is not scientific in principle, there is actually a scientific law that confirms that evolution is false. This scientific law is the second law of thermodynamics, which is also known as the law of entropy.

The first law of thermodynamics states that the total amount of energy in the universe is constant. It can change from one form to another, but it cannot be destroyed, and new energy cannot be created.

The second law of thermodynamics teaches that over time, the amount of usable energy is decreasing, and the amount of unusable energy is increasing. Put another way, the law of entropy teaches that when this reality and everything in it is left to its own devices over time without any intelligent intervention whatsoever, it will naturally wear down, break down, and fall into disorder.

This is why when you leave a car out in a field and don't do anything to it, it will rust and deteriorate over time. This is also why if you don't regularly maintain a house and you just let it sit there over a long period of time, it will deteriorate and fall apart all on its own. This is also why natural selection can only reshuffle information that already exists or eliminate information, and why it cannot create new information that did not previously exist. The law of entropy reigns supreme.

The second law of thermodynamics is so supreme that Authur Eddington, a contemporary of Albert Einstein, said the following:

"The practical measure of the random element which can increase in the universe but can never decrease is called entropy. Measuring by entropy is the same as measuring by the chance explained in the last paragraph, only the unmanageably large numbers are transformed (by a simple formula) into a more convenient scale of reckoning. Entropy continually increases. We can, by isolating parts of the world and postulating rather idealised conditions in our problems, arrest the increase, but we cannot turn it into a decrease. That would involve something much worse than a violation of an ordinary law of Nature, namely, an improbable coincidence. The law that entropy always increases-the second law of thermodynamics-holds, I think, the supreme position among the laws of Nature. If someone points out to you that your pet theory of the universe is in disagreement with Maxwell's equations-then so much the worse for Maxwell's equations. If it is found to be contradicted by observation-well, these experimentalists do bungle things sometimes. But if your theory is found to be against the second law of thermodynamics I can give you no hope; there is nothing for it but to collapse in deepest humiliation." (31)

As Eddington so eloquently put it, if a scientific theory or hypothesis contradicts the law of entropy, then it is impossible for said theory or hypothesis cannot possible be true, and must be consigned to collapse into the dust bin of history as a failed theory or hypothesis.

How does evolution contradict the law of entropy? It's quite simple. Evolution teaches that when the universe itself and everything in it is left to its own devices over time without any intelligent intervention, it naturally becomes more complex and ordered.

The law of entropy, as we saw earlier, teaches that when the universe itself and everything in it is left to its own devices over time without any intelligent intervention whatsoever, it naturally wears down, breaks down, and falls into disorder.

Evolution and the law of entropy are literally the opposite of each other. Since the law of entropy is such an irrefutable fact of science that it holds the supreme position among the laws of nature, this means that evolution is false, and cannot possibly be true from a scientific basis.

Atheists and evolutionists will try to get around this by saying that the law of entropy only applies to closed systems, and the earth is an open system, so this allows evolution and the law of entropy to exist at the same time. The problem is that the experiments that verified the law of entropy were performed on earth, so this would mean that the law of entropy works on open systems as well as closed ones. Plus even if it were true that the law of entropy only worked on closed systems, this would mean that the universe itself is a closed system since the law of entropy is in effect no matter where we look inside the universe.

Since evolution doesn't qualify as science due to it not being able to be verified or falsified by the scientific method, since evolution blatantly contradicts the law of entropy, and since evolutionists are trying to use science to get us to believe in a worldview that has multiple fatal flaws in its paradigm of history, this means that any so-called scientific evidence that atheists & evolutionists present to us cannot possibly support their worldview, and you can dismiss them if you don't want to deal with them for whatever reason. Of course, if you want to see responses to the so-called pieces of scientific evidence that atheists and evolutionists throw at us, there are many different creationist ministries that have dealt with their so-called evidence.

Now that we've dealt with that, it is time to discuss an irrefutable truth that is supported by mountains of evidence: Atheists are the most religious people on planet earth, and they project themselves onto Christians and creationists in order to condemn them.

ATHEISTS DENY EVERYTHING THEY OBSERVE IN REALITY

If you've been involved in the creation vs evolution debate for any significant length of time, then you've probably heard many an atheist claim that young earth creationists have to reject everything they know about science, geology, paleontology, astronomy, etc in order to justify their worldview. The truth of the matter is that atheists are the ones who have to deny everything they observe in reality in order to justify their worldview.

On page one of his 1987 book *The Blind Watchmaker*, atheist Richard Dawkins wrote the following:

"Biology is the study of complicated things that give the appearance of having been designed for a purpose." (32)

Dawkins starts out his book by admitting that all of biology, and ultimately all of reality, has the appearance of design. Dawkins then, of course, proceeds to spend the rest of the book trying to explain how biology and reality itself are not actually designed.

On June 24, 2017, Professor Stick put out a video titled "Another Creationist Claims The Universe Was Created". In this video, a creationist YouTuber called "A Voice In The Desert" said that a flower was evidence of intelligent design. In this video, Professor Stick said the following:

"So your argument here basically, 'Oh Look! A Flower! It's pretty, therefore a god.' Come on, man, you got to think of something better than that. That's, like, one of the things that atheists make fun of theists for. This exact argument? Don't ignore the fact that science has a completely sound explanation for this kind of stuff. A flower may seem to be designed because of how nice it looked, but design isn't the only way you can achieve something like that." (33)

As we can see, even modern day evolutionist YouTubers like Professor Stick admit that things like the flower, and ultimately all of reality, has the appearance of design, but then in the next breath they will claim that flowers and all of reality really aren't designed because of evolution, deep time, and big bang cosmology.

All the evolutionists and atheists out there who make this argument have to answer the following question:

What is the difference, practically speaking, between an

earth and universe that appears to be designed, but really isn't, and an earth & universe that appears to be designed because it is?

The correct answer, of course, is that there is literally no difference between the two. In both cases, everything appears to be designed. Since this is the case, since everything in reality has the appearance of design, we can safely conclude that it was designed by an intelligent designer, such as God.

What is funny about this particular dilema is that both the atheist camp and the young earth creationist camp acknowldge that reality has the appearance of design as far as they can observe. What seperates the two camps is that the young earth creationist camp says "reality appears to be designed, therefore it must be!" The atheist camp, on the other hand, says "All reality appears to be designed, but it really isn't because of evolution!"

This is not surprising though. Atheists and evolutionsts are the kind of people who will literally throw out all of reality if all of reality points towards intelligent design being true. In a 1999 article in *Nature* titled "A view from kansas on that evolution debate", Scott C Todd wrote the following:

"Even if all the data point to an intelligent designer, such an hypothesis is excluded from science because it is not

naturalistic. Of course the scientist, as an individual, is free to embrace a reality that transcends naturalism." (34)

The young earth creationist camp is the camp whose worldview actually conforms to reality, while the atheist camp acknowledges that they deny what they observe in reality to justify their worldview, and they will throw out all observable evidence in reality if they have to.

ATHEISTS FALSELY CLAIM THAT ATHEISM IS THE DEFAULT POSITION

In this same thread, there are many atheists out there who claim that atheism is the default position. By this, what they mean is that everyone is an atheist when they are born, and the only way people can believe in God, the biblical worldview, or religion in general is that they have to be indoctrinated into it as they grow up in their childhood and formative years. This, of course, is the opposite of what we observe in reality.

On March 31, 2016, *The Guardian* put out an article titled "Evolution Makes Scientific Sense. So Why Do Many People Reject It?" It is in this article where we read the following:

"Evolution is poorly understood by students and, disturbingly, by many of their science teachers. Although it is part of the compulsory science curriculum in most schools in the UK and the USA, more than a third of people in both countries reject the theory of evolution outright or believe that it is guided by a supreme being.

It is critical that the voting public have a clear understanding of evolution. Adaptation by natural selection, the primary mechanism of evolution, underpins a raft of current social concerns such as antibiotic resistance, the impact of climate change and the relationship between genes and environment. So why, despite formal scientific education, does intelligent design remain so intuitively plausible and evolution so intuitively opaque? And what can we do about it?

Developmental psychologists have identified two cognitive biases in very young children that help to explain the popularity of intelligent design. The first is a belief that species are defined by an internal quality that cannot be changed (psychological essentialism). The second is that all things are designed for a purpose (promiscuous teleology). These biases interact with cultural beliefs such as religion but are just as prevalent in children raised in secular societies.

Importantly, these beliefs become increasingly entrenched, making formal scientific instruction more and more difficult as children get older."

Child psychology studies have shown that intelligent design, and ultimately theism, are intuitive and plausible to human beings, even when they are raised in secular societies and households. Put another way, when human beings come out of the womb and they observe the reality around them, belief in intelligent design and theism is intuitive, natural, and what they logically conclude when they see all the design in reality.

On the other hand, evolution, contrary to what atheists and evolutionists say, is intuitively opaque. In other words, when human beings come out of the womb and observe the reality around them, atheistic evolution is not intuitive, it is not natural, and it is not what they logically conclude when they observe all the design in reality.

Simply put, child psychology studies show that intelligent design and theism is the default position in human beings when they come out of the womb, and it's the atheistic evolutionary worldview that you have to be indoctrinated into in order to believe it.

Obviously, since *The Guardian* is an anti-Christian publication, they did not like the conclusion of child psychology studies. So what did this article propose doing about it? We find out in the last three paragraphs in the article:

"Evolution is typically taught to students at around 14- to 15-years of age as they prepare for their GCSEs. After persistent lobbying by the British Humanist Association, evolution was included in the British national primary curriculum for the first time last year. From September 2015, students will be taught about evolution from Year 6, at around 10-11 years of age.

Might this still be too late? Kelemen chose 5- to 8-year-olds to test because at this age promiscuous teleology and psychological essentialism are still separate and fragmentary. She argues that by 10 years of age they have coalesced into a coherent theoretical framework that then gets in the way of contradictory scientific explanations and may remain the default, gut reaction, even in adults.

Her storybook works because it provides children with an alternative explanatory framework before these cognitive biases become entrenched. Her findings show that even very young children can understand the basic mechanisms of natural selection and can generalise that analogy to new examples. If part of the reason that intelligent design is so popular is because it seems intuitively correct, might the solution be to disrupt those intuitions very early on? Should we reconsider the national curriculum (yet again) and start teaching evolution even earlier?" (35)

The proposed solution by *The Guardian* is that we simply need to shovel atheistic evolutionary propaganda down the throats of children in the form of storybooks when those children are 5-8 years old. The reason why we should be doing this is because at that age, children do not have the cognitive abilities to challenge us and determine for themselves whether we are telling them the truth or not, so their natural and intuitive beliefs in intelligent design and theism can be overridden with enough indoctrination.

This proposed solution proves beyond a shadow of a doubt that atheism is not the default position that everyone is born into, and it proves conclusively that atheism is a religion that you have to be indoctrinated into.

The sickest part about this proposed solution is that I have personally seen atheists on the internet claim that

Christians are not allowed to raise their 5-8 year-old children in the ways of the Lord because the children don't have to cognitive abilities to challenge what we're telling them or determine for themselves whether we are right or wrong, and yet when it comes the atheistic worldview, these same people say that a child's lack of cognitive abilities is the exact reason why we should be indoctrinating them into the atheistic evolutionary worldview at that age.

Denying everything they observe in reality in order to justify their worldview is the way of the atheist.

ATHEISTS ILLEGITIMATELY REJECT CREATIONISM BECAUSE IT CANNOT BE VERIFIED BY OBSERVATIONAL SCIENCE

There are many atheists out there who reject young earth creationism as a possible explanation of origins because young earth creationism cannot be proven true with observational science in the present. However, when they make this argument, they are not only employing a double-standard, but they are also making an argument that is considered invalid by evolutionist authority figures of the past.

In the 45th issue of *American Scientist*, the late

evolutionist Theodosius Dobzhansky wrote an article titled "ON METHODS OF EVOLUTIONARY BIOLOGY AND ANTHROPOLOGY: Part I. Biology". In this article, Dobzhansky wrote the following:

"On the other hand, it is manifestly impossible to reproduce in the laboratory the evolution of man from the australopithecine, or of the modern horse from an Eohippus, or of a land vertebrate from a fish-like ancestor. These evolutionary happenings are unique, unrepeatable, and irreversible. It is as impossible to turn a land vertebrate into a fish as it is to effect the reverse transformation. The applicability of the experimental method to the study of such unique historical processes is severely restricted before all else by the time intervals involved, which far exceed the lifetime of any human experimenter.

And yet, it is just such impossibility that is demanded by antievolutionists when they ask for 'proofs' of evolution which they would magnanimously accept as satisfactory. This is about as reasonable a demand as it would be to ask an astronomer to recreate the planetary system, or to ask an historian to reenact the history of the world from Caesar to Eisenhower." (36)

So according to Dobzhansky, the evolution paradigm of

history cannot be verified by observational science via the scientific method. Because of this, Dobzhansky states that it is unreasonable for creationists to demand evidence from observational science that supports the truthfulness of evolution, which also implies that it is not valid for creationists to reject evolution simply because it cannot be proven true with observational science.

So according to atheists, rejecting young earth creationism as an explanation of origins because young earth creationism cannot be proven true with observational evidence is a valid argument, but if young earth creationists ask for observational evidence supporting evolution, or if young earth creationists reject evolution because it cannot be proven true with observational science, the demand and argument of young earth creationists is unreasonable and invalid! Apparently young earth creationists are not allowed to hold evolution to the same standard to which atheists and evolutionists hold young earth creationists.

In a 1975 issue of *Perspectives In Biology And Medicine*, evolution theorist C. Leon Harris wrote an article titled "An Axiomatic Interpretation of the Neo-Darwinian Theory of Evolution". It is in this article that Harris wrote the following:

"The axiomatic nature of the neo-Darwinian theory places the debate between evolutionists and creationists in a new perspective. Evolutionists have often challenged creationists experimental proof that species have been fashioned de novo. *Creationists have often demanded that evolutionists show how chance mutations can lead to adaptability, or to explain why natural selection has favored some species but not others with special adaptations, or why natural selection allows apparently detrimental organs to persist. We may now recognize that neither challenge is fair. If the neo-Darwinian theory is axiomatic, it is not valid for creationists to demand proof of the axioms, and it is not valid for evolutionists to dismiss special creation as unproved so long as it is stated as an axiom."* (37)

For those who do not know, an axiom is a concept that can neither be proved nor tested with observational science. With that in mind, what Harris saying here is that both evolution and young earth creationism are religious worldviews that cannot be proven true or even tested by observational science. Because this is the case, Harris says not only that it is invalid for creationists to demand evidence from observational science that supports the truthfulness of evolution, but Harris also says that it is equally invalid for evolutionists to reject young earth creationism on the basis that young earth creationism has not been proven true by

104

observational science!

The atheist and evolutionist authority figures of the past, it turns out, rightly understood that both atheistic evolution and young earth creationism were religious worldviews that cannot be proven true by observational science, and they also pointed out that it was invalid for their fellow evolutionists to reject young earth creationism simply because young earth creationism can't been proven true by observational science.

And yet, because today's atheists and evolutionists are completely ignorant of the history and what their founders and past authority figures said and wrote, they reject young earth creationism on the basis that it can't be proven true by observational science, an argument that was rejected as invalid by atheists and evolutionist authority figures decades ago.

ATHEISTS REJECT EVIDENCE THAT CONTRADICTS THEIR WORLDVIEW

There are many atheists out there who claim that young earth creationists accept or reject evidence based on whether or not it conforms to their worldview. Considering that atheists literally deny everything they observe in reality in order to justify their own worldview, it comes as no surprise that atheists are the ones who accept or reject evidence based on whether or not it conforms to their own worldview.

On September 27, 2020, Professor Stick uploaded a video to his YouTube channel titled "Creationist Debunks New Evidence Of Abiogenesis". In the video, we see Professor Stick say the following:

> "That would actually be very interesting. The components of life are supposed to have come about gradually, with the first step being something of a psuedo-life. That would be the most probable since it conforms to what we know about organic chemistry, but if real scientific research shows that life could have come about all at once, I am all down to consider it. Give me the paper, and I'll give it a read. See how my reaction to this is different than those of creationists? Scientists would consider this ideal, while creationists would accept or reject this idea immediately depending on if it conforms to their creationist myth." (38)

As we can see, Professor Stick claims that young earth creationists accept or reject scientific evidence on the basis of whether or not it conforms to their worldview. As we go through the video, we see professor stick read out loud a section of a *NewScientist* article that says that new scientific evidence shows that life came into existence fully-formed, and all at once. In response to this claim, we see Professor Stick say the following in the same video:

"What we do know is that it took a long period of time to develop, which is why I'm skeptical of the claim that the components of life all came about together at once." (39)

In reference to the new scientific evidence that life came into existence fully-formed all at once, Professor Stick claims that "we know" that it took a long period of time for life to develop, and this allows him to be skeptical of this new scientific evidence. In other words, Professor Stick is rejecting this new scientific evidence that shows at life came into existence fully-formed all at once because it does not conform to his atheistic, evolutionary worldview, the very thing that he accuses young earth creationists of doing.

On March 17, 2019, Professor Stick uploaded a video to his YouTube channel titled "More Creationist Arguments Against The Big Bang." In this video, there is a part where the creationist YouTuber "Freedom In God" points out that Paul Steinhardt, one of the founders of inflation theory, said that inflation theory had no observational evidence supporting it, and that inflation theory was based on unprovable assumptions. It is in this video where we see Professor Stick say the following in response:

"Ok, you can't just say, 'well look, this one particular physicist has a few problems with inflation, therefore inflation altogether is false.' Not only is that an appeal to authority, it's also just lazy." (40)

As we can see, Professor Stick's response to Steinhardt was to pretend that Steinhardt was just some random, johnny-come-lately physicist who dissents from inflation theory, and claim that it's illegitimate to reject inflation theory just because one physicist does.

The problem with this is that Steinhardt is not just some Johnny-come-lately physicist; he is literally one of the founders of inflation theory. When one of the founders of inflation theory admits that inflation theory has no observational evidence supporting it, and that it's based on unprovable assumptions, this means that inflation theory is most likely false. But because inflation theory conforms to his worldview, Professor Stick rejects Steinhardt's confession that inflation theory is has no observational evidence supporting it even though Steinhardt is in a postion as a co-founder of inflation theory to know better than Professor Stick.

I know that I am singling out Professor Stick on this issue, but considering that Professor Stick has over 200,000 subscribers to his YouTube channel, and considering that I've seen other atheists & evolutionsts behave like him, it's safe to say that atheists in general tend to reject any scientific evidence as well as any and all scientists that do not conform to their worldview, an acussation that Professor Stick and other atheists level at young earth creationists.

ATHEISTS ARE VINDICTIVE, AUTHORITARIAN CRY-BULLIES

If you've been on the internet for years like I have, then you've probably seen atheists and evolutionists claim that Christians and creationists are a bunch of hate-filled bigots if Christians and creationists dissent from the atheists and evolutionists on anything. Of course, the reality of the situation is that atheists are the ones who are such hate-filled bigots towards young earth creationists that they turn into authoritarian cry-bullies in an attempt to get christians and young earth creationists deplatformed from society.

On June 7, 2019, the atheist YouTuber "Shannon Q" put out a video titled "Hate Preach The Next Generation". In this video, Shannon Q discusses the New Independent Fundamentalist Baptist (NIFB) movement and their hateful rhetoric towards the LGBT community. As the video progresses, Shannon Q plays a clip of Temple Baptist Church pastor Michael Johnson talking about how the PayPal account for the *Make America Straight Again* conference was terminated, and Shannon Q admits that she and the rest of the atheist/evolutionist community on YouTube were responsible for making that happen. It is in this video where Shannon Q says the following:

"I'm going to leave you with this: You can make a difference. You already have. We've already cut off the Make America Straight campaign's PayPal account. We can do it to the rest of them. They're in clear violation of the terms of service. We can prevent them from getting funding so that they can't buy their plaquerds, so that they can't book their accommodations, so that they cannot go to places where people are mourning the loss of their loved ones and celebrate their deaths, and advocate for more." (41)

Not only does Shannon Q take credit for getting the PayPal account of the *Make America Straight Again* conference shut down, but she encourages the rest of her community to help her deplatform the rest of the NIFB movement from PayPal so that members of the NIFB movement cannot donate money to their leaders, so that they cannot buy merchandise from the NIFB, so that they cannot book hotel & motel rooms, and so that they can restrict the ability of the NIFB to travel.

As someone who is familiar with the NIFB movement due to my study of Faithful Word Baptist Church pastor Steven Anderson, I have seen them claim that the LGBT community is the irredeemable scum of the earth, and that they should be executed by the government. Considering that the New Testament teaches that LGBT people can not only be redeemed, but that God can help them get rid of their desires, I stand against the NIFB movement's claim about the LGBT community, and I don't like them any more than Shannon Q does.

With that being said, even Shannon Q acknowledges in her video that the NIFB movement has never committed violence or threatened to commit violence against the LGBT community, and they have never encouraged others to do the same. I would also like to point out that to the best of my knowledge, the NIFB movement has never tried to deplatform people from PayPal or other mainstream sites, and the NIFB movement has never tried to prevent people from being able to receive donations from their fans, buying merchandise, booking hotels & motels, or traveling simply because those people dissent from their worldview.

Because Shannon Q believes in doing those things and is actively engaging in such behavior, she is an authoritarian, hate-filled bigot who is worse than the NIFB movement.

On August 18, 2019, Shannon Q did a livestream on her channel with her boyfriend and evolutionist YouTuber "Paulogia" titled "Ken Ham donates over $4000 to LGBT charity! Paulogia and Shannon Q Celebration!" In this video, Shannon Q admits that she hates Ken Ham, the founder of Answers In Genesis, so much for dissenting from her pro-LGBT ideology that she donated over $1,000 dollars to an LGBT organization in Kentucky in Ken Ham's name. It is in this livestream where we see Shannon Q say the following:

"Every time I get a notification email for somebody donated to the PayPal pool, I'm like, 'YAA! YES!! IT'S WORKING!! OH MY GOD IT'S WORKING!! OH MY GOD IT'S WORKING!! OH MY GOD IT'S WORKING!!' I was really excited because I was very anxious when I did it. I was like, 'Oh my god! What if we only raise, like, 50 dollars?', but you guys killed it! Just blew it out of the park! Blew it out of the park! Exceeded every expectation I could have conceivably had! And now, instead of them being just hateful A—Holes, because of them, there's going to be gender-affirming care, and, uh, scholastic counseling, and counseling & support services provided to LGBT students at the University of Louisville in Kentucky, in Ken Ham's state, so Ken Ham's finally doing something good for Kentucky."
(42)

So according to Shannon Q, because she donated over $1,000 dollars to an LGBT organization in Ken Ham's name, it was the first time that Ken Ham has done anything good for the state of Kentucky, and by extension, the LGBT community.

It is pettiness like this that makes me wonder if Shannon Q is a nine-year-old inside an adult's body. When combined with her deplatforming the *Make America Straight Again* conference from PayPal, it's obvious that Shannon Q is a vindictive, authoritarian cry-bully who believes in deplatforming people who disagree with her worldview.

Speaking of authortitarian cry-bullies who belive in deplatforming people with whom they disagree with idea logically, let's take a look at something that her boyfriend, Paulogia, did.

On April 13, 2018, Paulogia uploaded a video to his channel titled "Atheist Banned From Ken Ham Event (Paulogia Denied)". In this video, Paulogia documents how he booked a reservation to attend the home school conference that the Alberta Home Education Association (AHEA) was hosting on April 13, 2018 because Ken Ham was a confirmed speaker for the event. Paulogia also documents that he accepted an invitation from AIG to attend a private dinner that took place around the same time.

Paulogia then discusses how two days before the conference, he got a phone call from Calvin Smith, the executive director of AIG-Canada, informing Paulogia that his dinner reservation for the private dinner hosted by AIG had been rescinded. On the day of the conference, Paulogia was on his way to the conference when he got an email from the president of the AHEA five hours before the conference was supposed to start informing him that his reservation for the conference had been rescinded.

In his video, Paulogia complains about AIG employing bully tactics on him, but he omits a very important detail that destroys his victim narrative. In his video, we see Paulogia say the following:

"Ken has been deplatformed before, and he rightly complains about it. I'd defend Ken Ham's right to speak anywhere he is invited to do so." (43)

As we can see, Paulogia claims that he would defend Ken Ham's right to freedom of speech anywhere that he is invited to do so. What makes this claim ring hollow is that on November 8, 2017, the CBC put out an article titled "Top U.S. creationist's invitation as keynote speaker for Alberta homeschooling convention draws fire". It is in this article that we read the following:

"Calgarian Paul Ens says he walked away from his Christian faith after reading Ham's creationist literature and started a YouTube channel dedicated to debunking Ham's teachings.

'As a citizen of Alberta and a father, I'm very concerned that Ken Ham is being brought in on multiple levels — primarily that he is a science denier. He denies evolution, he denies the age of the Earth,' Ens said."

Paul Erns is Paulogia's real name, and the article contains a hyperlink that takes to straight to Paulogia's YouTube channel, so we can clearly see here Paulogia claiming that because Ken Ham denies evolution, deep time, and big bang cosmology, Ham is a science-denier. Later on in the article, Paulogia says this:

"He worries they'll buy Ham's curriculum at the conference.

"Unfortunately, Ken's material is so anti-science, anti-education, his entire ministry is based upon keeping people back and holding back ideas," Ens said."

As we can see from the quote above, Paulogia not only

doubles down on his claim that Ken Ham is a science-denier, but he accuses Ken Ham of being anti-education, and of trying hold back people and their ideas.

Paulogia said the following about the AHEA's decision to book Ken Ham as a speaker:

"He says the fact Alberta's Home Education Association has booked Ham to speak raises questions.

'It signals to me that this homeschool group is not serious about following provincial curriculum or proper science education for their children,' he said." (44)

So not only does Paulogia declare that Ken Ham is anti-science and anti-education, but he also condemned the AHEA by claiming that their decision to book Ken Ham as a speaker shows that they do not take children's education seriously, especially with regard to science.

Paulogia's accusations toward Ken Ham and AHEA is a tactic that atheists and leftists use to get christians and conservatives deplatformed from speaking engagements and presentations that they get booked for at various organizations. The way the tactic works is that if a Christian or conservative gets booked to speak somewhere, the atheists and leftists will go to the organization and claim that the person they booked is a hate-filled bigot, a racist, homophobic, islamaphobic, neo-nazi, white supremacist, far-right, anti-science, etc. In too many cases, when the organization is told this by the atheists and leftists, they respond by canceling the speaking engagements of the Christian or conservative speaker that the atheists and leftists made these claims about.

Paulogia can claim all he wants that he defends Ken Ham's right to speak when he's invited to do so, but the fact of the matter is that five months prior to this AHEA conference taking place, Paulogia engaged in a bullying tactic that was designed to get Ken Ham's speaking engagement with the AHEA canceled, and he engaged in this tactic with *CBC News*. This was more than enough justification for AiG and AHEA to not allow Paulogia to attend their respective events because along with freedom of speech, we also have freedom of association, and we don't have to allow people who demonize us publicly to attend our events.

In his video about this, Paulogia said the following in response to Ken Ham:

"Why not welcome me with open arms to show me that

everything I heard is unjustified? Put your thoughts out there in the maket place of ideas and show me I'm wrong?" (45)

Paulogia challenges Ken Ham to put his young earth creationism beliefs out there into the public marketplace of ideas, but how is Ken Ham supposed to do that when Paulogia engages in cancel culture tactics when Ken Ham gets booked to speak somewhere?

While I readily acknowledge that not all atheists are authoritarian cry-bullies, there are many atheists who are, and Paulogia and Shannon Q serve as perfect examples of what that looks like in action.

ATHEIST HYPOCRISY ABOUT EDUCATIONAL BACKGROUND

There are many atheists out there who are quick to point out that many young earth creationists, myself included, who talk about scientific topics and criticize evolutionist scientists are unqualified to do so because we don't have scientific backgrounds or a scientific education background.

What makes this whole thing hypocritical is that most atheists and evolutionists that you see on YouTube and the internet do not have science backgrounds or science educational backgrounds, and yet they not only talk about scientific topics, but they also criticize creationists who do have scientific educational backgrounds and science degrees. Rules for me, not for thee.

This is similar to a situation where an evolutionist user on YouTube who followed me over to my BitChute channel commented on one of my videos, and he told me that because I encouraged people to subscribe to my channel at the end of my videos, and because I encouraged people to financially donate to TTOR through various crowd-funding platforms if they felt led to, this was proof that I was only in it for money, popularity, and attention.

This claim is completely hypocritical because a lot of atheist & evolutionist YouTubers literally do exactly the same thing. They encourage people to subscribe to their channels, check out their other videos, and they encourage people to donate to them via various crowd-funding platforms if they feel like it.

Apparently, when atheists and evolutionist content

creators do this, it's ok and morally acceptable, but if a creationist content creator does literally the exact same thing, they are bad and evil people for doing so.

FINAL THOUGHTS ON
ATHEISTIC EVOLUTION

As we can see from this chapter, atheistic evolution is nothing more than a religious worldview that does not qualify as science in principle. It's literally against observational science, it's based on making improvable assumptions, and it's adherents inevitably end up becoming authoritarian cry-bullies who want to censor and deplatform anyone who disagrees with them.

Things are so bad for the atheists and evolutionsts that they now refuse to have formal debates with young earth creationists in college or university settings.

In a 1996 article for *The Sciences* titled "Monkey Business", evolutionist Eugenie Scott wrote the following:

"If your local campus Christian fellowship asks you to 'defend evolution,' please decline. Public debates rarely change many minds; creationists stage them mainly in the

hope of drawing large sympathetic audiences. Have you ever watched the Harleem Globetrotters play the Washington Federals? The Federals get off some good shots, but who remembers them? The purpose of the game is to see the Globetrotters beat the other team.

And you will probably get beaten. In such a forum, scientific experts often try to pack a semester-long course into an hour, hoping to convey the huge sweep of evolution, the towering importance of its ideas, the masses of evidence in its favor. Creationist debaters know better. They come well-prepared with an arsenal of crisp, clear, superficially attractive antievolutionary arguments—fallacious ones, yes, but far too many for you to answer in the time provided. Even if you win the debate in some technical sense, most of the audience will still walk away from it convinced that your opponent has a great new science that the schools should hear about. Teachers have enough problems. Above all else, do no harm." (46)

According to Eugenie Scott, atheists and evolutionists cannot defeat young earth creationists in a formal debate, and so atheists and evolutionists should just avoid the debates altogether. Scott then provides three reasons why they cannot beat young earth creationists in a debate.

The first reason Scott lists is that there is so much evidence supporting evolution that atheists are unable to condense it all down into an hour-long debate. This reason is very weak because if there truly is an overwhelming amount of evidence supporting evolution, then you don't have to condense it all into an hour-long debate. You simply need to grab your 3-5 best pieces of evidence supporting evolution, and talk about those in the debate.

The second reason Scott gives is that creationists will pack so many fallacious arguments into a short amount of time that the atheists do not have enough time to respond to each and every single argument. The tactic of packing a whole bunch of arguments into a short amount of time for the purpose of not allowing your opponent to have enough time to answer all of them is called the Gish Gallop technique by atheists because atheists claim that the late creationist Duane Gish constantly used this tactic.

Having done some studying into the late Duane Gish, I find it incredibly unlikely that Dr. Gish ever employed the tactic of packing a bunch of arguments into a short amount of time for the purpose of not allowing his debate opponent enough time to respond to all his arguments. The reason that I find this highly unlikely is because back in 2002, Dr. Gish put out a six-part video debate workshop titled *Winning The Creation Debate*. In the booklet that accompanied the video series, we find that Dr. Gish wrote the following:

"Choose the most important subjects to be covered.

Limit number of subjects to be discussed—be strict!

Don't stray, don't allow opponent to drag you off into discussing peripheral material" (47)

As we can see in the quote above, Dr. Duan Gish instructed his fellow creationists to limit the amount of topics they talked about in debates with evolutionists, and he instructed them to make the few topics they talk about in the debate to be the most important topics related to the creation versus evolution debate. Gish also instructed creationists to not allow evolutionists to go off into other unrelated topics, and to keep the evolutionists on-topic.

This is damming to the atheists and evolutionists because they claimed that Dr. Gish only won so many debates because he would pack so many arguments about so many topics into such a short amount of time that his evolutionist opponents wouldn't have the proper time to respond, and yet when we looked at what Dr. Gish instructed creationists to do in debates against evolutionists in order to win those debates, Dr. Gish actually instructed creationists to do the opposite.

If Gish was the one in debates with evolutionists who was packing a whole bunch of arguments and topics into such a short amount of time that there was not enough time for the atheists and evolutionists to respond to all of them, then why was Gish telling his fellow creationists that they needed to keep atheists and evolutionists on-topic, and not let them go off into unrelated topics?

The answer is that atheists and evolutionists are the ones who will pack a bunch of different arguments and topics in such a short amount of time that their debate opponent cannot possibly answer all of them in the time allotted, and when their opponent fails to answer every single thing the evolutionists and atheists say, the evolutionists and atheists arbitrarily declare themselves the winner of said debate. This was my experience when arguing with atheists and evolutionists on Facebook when I was younger.

The only person that I have ever seen advocate using the so-called Gish Gallop technique for the purpose of defeating an opponent in a debate was the well-known atheist Bill Nye. In the May/June 2014 issue of *Skeptical Inquirer*, atheist Bill Nye wrote the following about his 2014 debate with Ken Ham:

"Those of you familiar with creationism and its followers are familiar with the remarkable Duane Gish (no longer living—at least as far as we know). His debating technique came to be known as the "Gish Gallop." He was infamous for jumping from one topic to another, introducing one spurious or specious fact or line of reasoning after another. A scientist debating Gish often got bogged down in details and, by all accounts, came across looking like the loser.

It quickly occurred to me that I could do the same thing. If you make the time to watch the debate (let's say for free at , wink), I hope you'll pick up on this idea. I did my best to slam Ken Ham with a great many scientific and common sense arguments. I believed he wouldn't have the time or the focus to address many of them." (48)

Even though atheists like Eugenie Scott consider the Gish Gallop technique to be a fallacious debate tactic, this did not stop Bill Nye from using the tactic against Ken Ham in his 2014 debate with Ken Ham, and this is according to Bill Nye's own words. Apparently, according to Bill Nye, using the Gish

Gallop technique is perfectly ok if you're an atheist and evolutionist, but if a creationist were to use the Gish Gallop technique against an atheist, that would be immoral and fallacious.

The third reason that Eugenie Scott gives is that even if the evolutionist wins the debate, the fact that a debate was held will give students and viewers the impression that there is legitimate evidence supporting young earth creationism. This reason is the most valid that Eugenie Scott gave because it shows that the thought of a single student rejecting evolution in favor of young earth creationism based on evidence is so abhorrent to her that she would rather not allow young earth creationism to present its case in the public education system.

We see Eugenie Scott confirm this fear on page 23 of *Where Darwinism Meets The Bible*, where Eugenie Scott said the following:

"'In my opinion,' she writes. 'using creation and evolution as topics for critical-thinking exercises in primary and secondary schools is virtually guaranteed to confuse students about evolution and may lead them to reject one of the major themes in science.'" (49)

Not only do atheists and evolutionists want to prevent students and young people from seeing the evidence for young earth creationism, but they are even willing to lie to students about the evidence for evolution in order to get young people to become evolutionists instead of creationists.

On August 25, 2008, evolutionist Bora Zivkovic wrote an article for *ScienceBlogs* titled "Why Teaching Evolution Is Dangerous." It is in this article that Zivkovic writes the following:

"Mr. Campbell knows how tricky this process is. You cannot bludgeon kids with truth (or insult their religion, i.e., their parents and friends) and hope they will smile and believe you. Yes, NOMA is wrong, but is a good first tool for gaining trust. You have to bring them over to your side, gain their trust, and then hold their hands and help them step by step. And on that slow journey, which will be painful for many of them, it is OK to use some inaccuracies temporarily if they help you reach the students.

If a student, like Natalie Wright who I quoted above, goes on to study biology, then he or she will unlearn the inaccuracies in time. If most of the students do not, but those cutesy examples help them accept evolution, then it is OK if they keep some of those little inaccuracies for the rest of their lives. It is perfectly fine if they keep thinking that Mickey Mouse evolved as long as they think evolution is fine and dandy overall. Without Mickey, they may have become Creationist activists instead. Without belief in NOMA they would have never accepted anything, and well, so be it. Better NOMA-believers than Creationists, don't you think?" (50)

There are so many things wrong with what Zivkovic said. The first one is that according to Zivkovic, getting students to accept evolution is more important than telling them the truth; it is ok to lie to students if doing so will get them to believe in evolution. Furthermore, it's considered just fine to Zivkovic if the students end up believing in lies the rest of their lives, as long as they believe in evolution the whole time.

If a young earth creationist said that getting students to accept young earth creationism was more important than telling the students the truth, and that it was ok to lie to students about the evidence for young earth creationism as long as they spent the rest of their lives believing in young earth creationism, do you think atheists and evolutionists would tolerate that for one second? Of course not! And yet they believe they're justified and righteous when they do literally that exact thing in order to get students to believe in atheistic evolution.

Secondly, this idea of lying in order to gain their trust to the point where they accept evolution sounds to me an awful lot like the concept of "lying for the Lord" that Mormons employ to convert people to their faith and keep them in the LDS church, except it's more like "lying for atheism". Truth doesn't mean a thing to Zivkovic.

Thirdly, Zivkovic acknowledges that without lying to students about evolution, those students might end up rejecting evolution and accepting creationism. He believes that it is better for students and people in general to believe in lies about evolution the rest of their lives than it is to believe in creationism, and ultimately the God of the Bible.

Zovkovic's blatant promotion of lying to students in order to get them to believe in atheistic evolution is so evil, immoral, and shameful that I am not surprised that he changed his account name on *ScienceBlogs* from "Bora Zivkovic" to "clock" a couple years ago to try and hide the fact that he wrote the article.

When I look at the fatally-flawed paradigm of history

that atheistic evolution presents us, and I see the religious hypocrisy, double-standards, and constant projection of themselves onto others that atheists and evolutions do, I find it amazing that Christians actually capitulate to these people.

When I look at how atheists are such authoritarian cry-bullies that they will shut down and censor all who dissent from their worldview, I find it astounding that Christians mesh their worldview with the biblical worldview and creates old earth creationism in an attempt to appease those atheists.

In the next chapter, we will deal with old earth creationism, and its adherents.

Chapter 3

Old Earth Creationism

THE HERETICAL COMPROMISE

When you look at the landscape of the young earth creationism movement, a lot of the focus has been on creation versus evolution, especially atheistic evolution. You see it all the time with the big young earth creationism ministries like *Answers in Genesis* and the *Institute for Creation Research*. As big of a threat to the biblical worldview as atheistic evolutionists are, old earth creationists constitute a far bigger threat to the biblical worldview than the atheists and evolutionists do.

Let's define some terms before we move on to explaining why old earth creationism is rank heresy.

DEFINING TERMS

Old earth creationism is the belief that God created the universe, the earth, the sea, and everything that is in those three things over the course of 14-16 billion years.

With this in mind, an old earth creationist is merely a person who believes in old earth creationism.

While some old earth creationists believe in deep time and big bang cosmology while rejecting evolution, there is a group of old earth creationists called theistic evolutionists who not only accept deep time and big bang cosmology, but they also accept evolution as the atheists teach it. In other words, theistic evolutionists accept everything that atheistic evolutionists say, and then claim that God is behind it all.

Many young earth creationists will tell you that old earth creationism is a compromise on the biblical worldview, and that old earth creationists are compromising on the Biblical worldview in order to appease the atheists and evolutionists. According to the Cambridge Dictionary, the word "compromise" as a verb means:

"to lower or weaken standards" (51)

When you tell someone that you don't have to believe

that Jesus was a miracle worker in order to be a true Jesus follower, you have lowered the standards of the biblical worldview. If you tell someone that you don't have to believe that Jesus is God the Son in order to be a true jesus follower, then you are lowering the standards and teachings of the biblical worldview.

Likewise, when you tell someone that you don't have to believe the straight-forward and contextual reading of the Bible in order to be an orthodox believer, and that you can reinterpret the Bible in light of evolution, deep time, and big bang cosmology, that is lowering the standards of the biblical worldview.

A heresy is a belief or teaching that contradicts the official beliefs or teachings of a worldview. In the case of the biblical worldview, a heresy is a belief or teaching that contradicts the official beliefs or teachings that the Bible communicates regarding history, science, morality, sin, salvation, etc.

In turn, this means that a heretic is someone who believes in or teaches heresy. In relation to the biblical worldview, a heretic is a person whose belief or teaching contradicts the official beliefs or teachings of the biblical worldview.

Now that we've defined these terms, it's time to start getting into the evidence that old earth creationism is a heresy.

OLD EARTH CREATIONISTS VIEW THE SCIENTIFIC COMMUNITY AS A HIGHER AUTHORITY ON ORIGINS THAN THE BIBLE

One of the things that you hear old earth creationists say all the time is that young earth creationism is not based on a careful study of the Bible, and that young earth creationists simply don't understand things like hermeneutics, the English language, rules of interpretation, etc.

On pages 9-10 of his 2011 paper *When The Saints Go Marching In (Matthew 27:52-53): Historicity, Apocalyptic Symbol, and Biblical Inerrancy*, old earth creationist Mike Licona said the following:

"This confusion between inerrancy and hermeneutics is clearly illustrated in theological debates over interpreting the creation account in Genesis. Al Mohler who takes a young earth view of Genesis contends that the theological costs of the old earth view held by Geisler are difficult to reconcile with a historical Adam in Genesis and Romans. Other young earthers often accuse old earthers of denying the inerrancy of the text." (52)

As we can see, Licona claims that young earth creationists believe in young earth creationism because they don't understand how hermeneutics work.

On page 160 of his book *7 Reasons Why You Can Trust The Bible*, old earth creationist Erwin Lutzer said the following:

"The so-called conflict between science (the physical creation) and religion (the spiritual re-creation) simply does not exist. It is impossible for the Bible to contradict science since God is the author of both. If we are pressed to explain generations of conflict, the answer is (1) that those who believe the Bible have often crafted interpretations that were not based on a careful study of the text. Needless to say, the earth was not created in 4004 BC as the study notes in one Bible affirm. Many of us hold to a "young earth", but since the Bible does not tell us when God created the heavens and the earth, we must respect those who believe that the earth is much older than some creationists have believed." (53)

So according to Lutzer, not only does the Bible not teach that the earth and universe are 6,000 years old, but young earth creationists who think that the Bible does teach that have not carefully studied the Bible.

Back in 2014, there was a video uploaded to a YouTube

channel called "Theology, Philosophy and Science" titled "William Lane Craig: Young Earth Creationism Is Embarrassing". In this video, we saw old earth creationist William Lane Craig directly address young earth creationism. Unfortunately, the "Theology, Philosophy and Science" YouTube channel was terminated by YouTube at some point in 2018 or 2019, so we no longer have access to that entire video.

Fortunately for us, on August 29, 2018, I uploaded a video to my BitChute channel titled "Debunking William Lane Craig's Arguments Against YEC (Justin Derby)". This video was my response to the "William Lane Craig: Young Earth Creationism Is Embarrassing" video. It is in this video where you see William Lane Craig say the following:

"Yes, I've seen a comparable statistic that says that over 50 percent of evangelical pastors think that the world is less than 10,000 years old. Now when you think about that Kevin, that is just hugely embarrassing that over half of our ministers really believe that the universe is only around 10,000 years old. This is just, scientifically, it's nonsense, and yet this is the view that the majority of our pastors hold; it's really quite shocking when you think about it." (54)

According to William Lane Craig, young earth creationism is embarrassing because it is scientific nonsense.

In other words, young earth creationism is embarrassing because it contradicts the majority opinion of the scientific and academic community on origins, which is evolution, billions of years, and big bang cosmology.

So according to old earth creationists, young earth creationism is embarrassing because it's scientific nonsense and is not based on a careful study of the biblical text, and young earth creationists are just a bunch of stupid hicks who don't understand hermeneutics, language, rules of interpretation, etc.

So if young earth creationists are interpreting the Bible wrong by accepting the straight-forward, contextual reading of it, then what is the proper way of interpreting the Bible according to old earth creationists?

On September 8, 2016, old earth creationist Frank Turek published an article on his ministry website titled "Why Andy Stanley Is Right About The Foundation Of Christianity And How To Defend It". It is in this article where we see Turek write the following:

"Sometimes we even use what we learn from nature or philosophy to overrule what appears to be the clear reading of Scripture. The rotation of the earth around the sun is one such example. Another is the immaterial nature of God. We

use the book of nature and the principles of human communication to realize that the Bible uses observational language to describe nature (sun rising and setting) and metaphors to describe God's attributes (He has eyes, arms, legs, etc.)." (55)

As we can see from the first sentence of this quote, Turek says that old earth creationists use what we learn from nature or philosophy to overrule the straight-forward, contextual reading of the Bible, especially on origins. It is very interesting to see Truek admit that they overrule the clear reading of scripture by reinterpreting it in light of philosophy. It's almost like they're re-interpreting the Bible in light of evolution and deep time!

Turek clarified this in a video that he uploaded to his *Cross Examined* YouTube channel on December 28, 2015 that was titled "How Old Is The Universe?" It is in this video where you see Truek say the following:

"The point here is, is the universe old? It may be old; it may be young. I don't think either are definitive, but if I had to guess, I'd say it's old because I don't think the laws of physics have changed. The bottom line is that God created is certainly more sure than when." (56)

So as we can see, Frank Turek admits that the universe

might be young. Why does he pay lip service to the possibility that young earth creationism is true? It's because the straight-forward and contextual reading of the Bible leads you to the conclusion that the earth and universe are 6,000 years old, as we saw in chapter one.

Despite his lip service to young earth creationism, Turek concludes that the universe is billions of years old. Does he say that he came to this conclusion because that's what a straight-forward reading of the Bible shows us? No. He comes to that conclusion because he reinterprets the Bible in light of evolution, deep time, and big bang cosmology.

Some old earth creationists might say that reinterpreting the Bible in light of evolution, deep time, and big bang cosmology is the correct way of interpreting the Bible, but as we are about to see, this idea is false.

When we return to my "Debunking William Lane Craig's Arguments Against YEC (Justin Derby)" video on my BitChute channel, we see William Lane Craig say the following:

"Well, I think with regard to Christian faith and practice, I would say you need first and foremost to do your biblical hermeneutics responsibly and objectively. You need to not interpret the Bible in light of modern science, but

interpret it according to what its original author and audience would have understood. That's the first and foremost task, is to interpret the Bible objectively and correctly.

Then the second task will be trying to integrate what we learn from the Bible with the worldview of modern science, so as to have a sort of synoptic worldview that takes into account all that we've learned, not only from divine revelation, but from God's revelation in nature, in the book of nature. And then we will build a synoptic sort of worldview that makes the best sense of the data." (57)

When we examine what William Lane Craig said here, we see two jaw-dropping revelations. The first one is that William Lane Craig has a Freudian slip and admits that old earth creationists reinterpret the Bible in light of the worldview of modern science, not the actual scientific data. This means that William Lane Craig and other old earth creationists are reinterpreting the Bible in light of the majority opinion of the scientific and academic community, which is evolution, billions of years, and big bang cosmology.

The second thing that William Lane Craig admits is even though we are not supposed to reinterpret the Bible in light of the worldview of modern science, old earth creationists like himself reinterpret the Bible in light of the worldview of modern science in order to make a synoptic worldview between the two.

In other words, William Lane Craig is saying that he and other old earth creationists reinterpret the Bible in light of evolution, billions of years, and big bang cosmology even though they know that they are not supposed to!

This is the ultimate form of intellectual dishonesty! William Lane Craig and other old earth creationists know full well that a straight-forward and contextual reading of the Bible leads you to the conclusion that the earth and universe are 6,000 years old, and they know that they are not supposed to reinterpret the Bible in light of evolution, deep time, and big bang cosmology. But because they view the majority opinion of the scientific and academic community as a higher authority on origins than God and the Bible, they reinterpret the Bible in light of evolution, deep time, and big bang cosmology, and they condemn young earth creationists for accepting the straight-forward reading of the Bible.

In case there is any doubt that old earth creationists view the majority opinion of the scientific and academic community as a higher authority on origins than God and the Bible, let me introduce you to a theistic evolutionist named

Perry Marshall. On page 327 of his 2015 book *Evolution 2.0*, Perry Marshall writes the following:

"Modern science speaks much more definitively about the age of the earth than the Bible does, so it is perfectly legitimate to allow science to settle this question." (58)

Most old earth creationists show by their actions that they view the majority opinion of the scientific and academic community as a higher authority than God and the Bible on the issue of origins, but they usually don't admit it publically. Not so with Perry Marshall; he is the only old earth creationist that I am aware of who has publically and in writing admitted to it.

OLD EARTH CREATIONISTS REJECT WHAT GOD SAYS ABOUT SCRIPTURAL INTERPRETATION

Old earth creationists know that a straight-forward and contextual reading of the Bible leads you to the conclusion that the earth and universe are 6,000 years old, and they know that almost all of the information that leads you to that conclusion is found in Genesis and Exodus, which were put together and written by Moses. Because of this, old earth creationists will try to convince you that God spoke to Moses in dreams or visions when he revealed his revelations to Moses, and they will say that God spoke to Moses in a coded language that, when properly interpreted, leads you to conclude that old earth creationism is true.

The problem with their claims is that it directly and completely contradicts what God said about his revelations to Moses in Numbers 12:6-9:

"he said, 'Listen to my words:

When there is a prophet among you, I, the Lord, reveal myself to them in visions, I speak to them in dreams. But this is not true of my servant Moses; he is faithful in all my house. With him I speak face to face, clearly and not in riddles; he sees the form of the Lord. Why then were you not afraid to speak against my servant Moses?'

The anger of the Lord burned against them, and he left them."

As we can see in this passage, God himself said that he did not speak to Moses in dreams or visions, but that he spoke to Moses face to face. God also says that he spoke to Moses clearly, and not in riddles. In other words, God says that when he revealed his revelations to Moses, he did speak to Moses in a straightforward manner, and he did not speak to Moses in any kind of coded language.

The irony here is just too rich and poetic. Old earth creationists claim that God spoke to Moses in dreams and visions when he revealed his revelations to Moses, but God himself specifically said that he did not speak to Moses in dreams or visions when he revealed his revelations to him. Old earth creationists claim that God did not speak to Moses in a straight-forward manner, and that God spoke to Moses in coded language, and yet God himself specifically said that he did speak to Moses in a straightforward manner, and that he did not speak in any kind of coded language to Moses.

By claiming that God revealed himself to Moses in dreams or visions, and claiming that God spoke to Moses in coded language, old earth creationists not only contradict Numbers 12:6-9, but they are teaching heresy.

GAP THEORY & DAY-AGE THEORY
CONTRADICT JESUS' WORDS

In order to cram billions of years into the Bible, old earth creationists will hold to either gap theory, or day-age theory.

gap theory is the idea that there is a gap between the

beginning of the earth & universe and the first day of creation, a gap that you can squeeze billions of years into. In this theory, the human race is only 6,000 years old, but the universe and earth are billions of years old.

Day-age theory is the idea that each of the days of creation are long periods of time instead of being ordinary days like we experience today. Since old earth creationists believe that the universe is 14-16 billion years old, the days of creation are periods of a couple billion years according to day-age theory.

The problem with both of these theories that old earth creationists have come up with is that God himself ruled out both theories in the old testament, and Jesus ruled both theories out in the New Testament.

In Exodus 20:8-11, we read the following:

"Remember the Sabbath day by keeping it holy. Six days you shall labor and do all your work, but the seventh day is a sabbath to the Lord your God. On it you shall not do any work, neither you, nor your son or daughter, nor your male or female servant, nor your animals, nor any foreigner residing in your towns. For in six days the Lord made the heavens and the earth, the sea, and all that is in them, but he rested on the seventh day. Therefore the Lord blessed the

Sabbath day and made it holy."

As we can see in the above passage, God himself said that he made the universe, the earth, the sea, and everything that is in those three things over the course of six ordinary days before resting on the seventh. This disproves gap theory because gap theory teaches that God made everything over the course of billions of years, not six ordinary days.

What God said in Exodus 20:8-11 also disproves day-age theory because God was talking in the context of the seven-day calendar week that we live through today. It makes no sense for God to say that the Israelites should work for six 24-hour days before resting on the seventh 24-hour day because God worked for six periods of millions of years before resting for a seventh period of millions of years. However, if God is telling them to work for six 24-hour days and rest on the seventh 24-hour day because he created the universe and everything in it in six 24-hour days before resting on the seventh 24-hour day, then it makes perfect sense because God is simply asking them to work as long as he did, essentially telling them to do something that he himself did.

In Mark 10:1-9, we read the following:

"Jesus then left that place and went into the region of Judea and across the Jordan. Again crowds of people came

to him, and as was his custom, he taught them.

Some Pharisees came and tested him by asking, 'Is it lawful for a man to divorce his wife?'

'What did Moses command you?' he replied.

They said, 'Moses permitted a man to write a certificate of divorce and send her away.'

'It was because your hearts were hard that Moses wrote you this law," Jesus replied. 'But at the beginning of creation God "made them male and female." "For this reason a man will leave his father and mother and be united to his wife, and the two will become one flesh." So they are no longer two, but one flesh. Therefore what God has joined together, let no one separate.'"

In the above passage, we can see Jesus teaching that male, female, and marriage at the beginning of creation. In order to understand how this teaching refutes gap theory and day-age Theory, let's examine when Adam, Eve, and marriage were created on each timeline.

According to the gap theory timeline of history, Adam,

Eve, and marriage were created 6,000 years ago on a 14-16 billion year timeline. That places the creation of Adam, Eve, and marriage virtually at the very end of the timeline, which is the opposite of the beginning of the timeline.

According to the day-age theory timeline, Adam, Eve, and marriage were created a couple billion years ago on a 14-16 billion year timeline. This places Adam and Eve's creation not as close to the end of the timeline as gap theory, but it's still absolutely nowhere near the beginning.

According to the young earth creationism timeline of history, Adam, Eve, and marriage were created on day six of a 6,000 year timeline of history. This places the creation of Adam, Eve, and marriage virtually at the very beginning of the timeline.

Which of these three timelines allows Jesus' teaching that male, female, and marriage were created at the beginning of creation to be true on a factual basis? The answer, of course, is the young earth creationism timeline of history; it's the only timeline that has the creation of Adam, Eve, and marriage at the beginning of creation. The gap theory and day-age theory timelines of history have Adam, Eve, and Marriage being created towards or at the end of their timelines of history.

Since old earth creationism teaches that Adam, Eve, and marriage were created at or towards the end of our timeline of history, and since the Bible teaches that Adam, Eve, and marriage were created at the beginning of creation, this means that old earth creationism is a heresy.

THE GENESIS 1:5 OBJECTION

Another objection that old earth creationists like to bring up is that they will claim that the word "day" in Genesis 1:5 is a 12-hour period of time, therefore the days of creation cannot be 24-hour periods of time like today. This obection fails because all you have to do is read the context preceding Genesis 1:5.

In Genesis 1:3-5, we read the following:

"And God said, 'Let there be light,' and there was light. God saw that the light was good, and he separated the light from the darkness. God called the light 'day,' and the darkness he called 'night.' And there was evening, and there was morning—the first day."

While it is true that there are no numbers or times of day attached to the word day in verse 5, you realize that this is all part of the first day of creation. When you read Genesis 1:1-5, you see that on the first day of creation, God created space, matter, time, the universe, the earth, and light. We also see God seperated the light from the darkness on the first day of creation. These is nothing in Genesis 1:5 that shows that the days of creation were anything other than ordinary days like we experience today.

THE GENESIS 2:4 OBJECTION

Another claim that old earth creationists like to make is that because the word "day" appears without any numbers or times of day attached to it in Genesis 2:4, then none of the days of the creation account could have been 24-hour days.

While the word "day" doesn't appear in the NIV version of the Bible, when we turn to the King James Version of Genesis 2:4, we read the following:

Genesis 2:4: *"These are the generations of the heavens and of the earth when they were created, in the day that the Lord God made the earth and the heavens."* (KJV)

When there are no numbers or times of day attached to the word "day", then the word is referring to a period of time longer than an ordinary day like way experience today. With that in mind, you could translate Genesis 2:4 to this:

"These are the generations of the heavens and of the earth when they were created, in the period of time that the Lord God made the earth and the heavens."

How long was that period of time where God made the earth and the heavens? According to Exodus 20:8-11, that period of time was six ordinary days like we experience today. There is absolutely nothing about Genesis 2:4 that proves that the days of creation are longer than the ordinary days we experience today.

THE VEGETATION ON THE THIRD DAY OF CREATION OBJECTION

Yet another objection that old earth creationists will make is that the third day of creation has to be longer than 24 hours because of the growth of vegetation and fruit-bearing plants. This objection is just plain silly when you look at what the text says.

On page 156 of his book *Judge Not*, Todd Friel wrote the following:

"The sixth letter of the Hebrew alphabet is waw (pronounced: vav). When placed in front of a word or phrase, it means "and then". When used with a past-tense verb, it means an action is completed 'and then' the next thing happens. This is called the waw consecutive." (59)

Let's turn to Genesis 1:11-13, and see if we can spot the waw consecutive:

"Then God said, 'Let the land produce vegetation: seed-bearing plants and trees on the land that bear fruit with seed in it, according to their various kinds.' And it was so. The land produced vegetation: plants bearing seed according to their kinds and trees bearing fruit with seed in it according to their kinds. And God saw that it was good. And there was evening, and there was morning—the third day."

As we can see in the passage, on the third day of creation, God essentially said, "let there be vegitation and fruit-bearing plants." In the next sentence after God finishes speaking, we see the phrase, "And it was so." This is the waw consecutive, and after the waw consecutive, we see vegitation and fruit-bearing plants come into existence. This means that the vegitation and fruit-bearing plants came into existence immediately after God spoke them into existence; there was no delay or prolongment in their coming into existence. It's pretty obevious that this can occur within an ordinary day like we experience today.

THE ADAM ANIMAL-NAMING OBJECTION

Another objection that old earth creationists will bring up is that they will claim that the sixth day of creation has to be longer than 24 hours because Adam had to name all the animals.

In his article "Naming the animals: all in a day's work for Adam", young earth creationist Russell Grigg wrote the following about this objection:

"There are 3,600 seconds in an hour, so Adam could have completed his task in under an hour. If he did it in a more leisurely and contemplative fashion, it would have taken a few hours at the most (excluding time out for 'coffee breaks'!). Surely a pleasant day's work, leaving plenty of time for God to create Eve from Adam's side that same afternoon." (60)

When you consider that Adam came pre-programmed straight from the hand of God, and that Adam was genetically perfect, Adam would have easily been able to name all the animals in the way that Griggs describes. The problem with old earth creationists is that they assume that the way human beings are today is the way they've always been, which is an assumption that comes from the atheistic evolutionary worldview.

THE HEBREW 4:3-5 OBJECTION

Another argument that old earth creationists make is that Hebrews 4:3-5 shows that the seventh day of creation hasn't ended yet, and we are still in it. As we'll see in a moment, this argument ignores the basic rules of the english language.

Not only does Hebrews 4:3-5 not say that we are currently in the seventh day of creation right now, but when you turn to Exodus 31:16-17, you read the following:

"The Israelites are to observe the Sabbath, celebrating it for the generations to come as a lasting covenant. It will be a sign between me and the Israelites forever, for in six days the Lord made the heavens and the earth, and on the seventh

day he rested and was refreshed.'"

As we can see in the above passage, the seventh day is referred to in the past tense. It does not say that God was resting and being refreshed in the seventh day; it says that God rested and was refreshed on the seventh day. In fact, in every instance where the seventh day of creation is referred to, it is always referred to in the past tense.

Past tense indicates that whatever is being referred to is a past event. Since the seventh day of creation is consistently referred to in the past tense in the Bible, this means that the seventh day of creation was a past event, and it is not an event that we are currently in today.

WHEN ALL ELSE FAILS FOR OLD EARTH CREATIONISTS

When all their scriptural arguments fail, old earth creationists will say that the fact that God created is more important than knowing when he created.

When old earth creationists make this claim, I have three questions for them:

If the fact that God created is more important than when God created, then why does God insist on defining the days of creation as ordinary days like we experience today in Exodus 20:8-11 and Exodus 31:16-17?

If the fact that God created is more important than when God created, then why does God give us genealogies and time spans that cover the entire time between the beginning of the earth and universe, and the fourth year of King Solomon's reign?

If the fact that God created is more important than when God created, then why does Jesus teach that male, female, and marriage were created at the beginning of creation in Mark 10?

In order to convince us that God isn't concerned with us knowing when he created all of reality and everything in it, old earth creationists have to provide satisfactory answers to those three questions. I am convinced that old earth creationists cannot provide satisfactory answers to those questions because if God wasn't concerned about letting us know when he made everything, he wouldn't have provided all the data we covered in chapter 1.

OLD EARTH CREATIONISM LEADS TO DENIAL OF BIBLICAL INNERANCY

Those of you reading this may be wondering to yourself, "if one rejects the young earth creationism timeline of history that the Bible teaches, what path does acceptance of old earth creationism take them? What is the logocial conclusion that such a path leads to?"

The answer is that if you follow old earth creationism to its logical conclusion, you will end up rejecting biblical inerrancy.

On page nine of his paper *When The Saints Go Marching In (Matthew 27:52-53): Historicity, Apocalyptic Symbol, and Biblical Inerrancy*, old earth creationist Mike Licona wrote the following:

"I hope it has become clear in this paper that my intent was not to dehistoricize a text that Matthew intended as historical. If I had, that would be to deny the inerrancy of the text. Instead, what I have done is to question whether

Matthew intended for the raised saints to be understood historically." (61)

Matthew 27:52-53 is the passage in Matthew where as soon as Jesus died, there was an earthquake, the tombs broke open, and dead people physicaly rose from the dead, and walked among the people in the city. Licona's thesis of his entire paper is that Matthew never intended this passage to be understood as a historical claim. In the quote above, Licona says that if Matthew actually did intend that passage to be understood as a historical claim, then he admits that he would be guilt of denying biblical inerrancy for suggesting otherwise.

When we examine Matthew 27:50-54, we read the following:

"And when Jesus had cried out again in a loud voice, he gave up his spirit.

At that moment the curtain of the temple was torn in two from top to bottom. The earth shook, the rocks split and the tombs broke open. The bodies of many holy people who had died were raised to life. They came out of the tombs after Jesus' resurrection and went into the holy city and appeared to many people.

When the centurion and those with him who were guarding Jesus saw the earthquake and all that had happened, they were terrified, and exclaimed, 'Surely he was the Son of God!'"

In the passage, we can clearly see it saying that after Jesus died, there was a big earthquake, the curtain of the temple was torn in two, and after the tombs broke open, many different holy people physically rose from the dead, walked into the city, and were seen by many people. But notice what verse 54 says: It specifically says that the centurion and those with him who were guarding Jesus saw these event happen, and that this is why they were terrified and excalimed that Jesus was the Son of God. Matthew clearly intended verses 52-53 to be understood as historical claims.

Matthew 27:54 literally refutes the thesis of Licona's paper, and yet when you read the entire paper, Licona never once mentions Matthew 27:54, not even in the section of the paper where he addresses his opponents' arguements. This shows a major lack of integrity and honesty on Licona's part.

Since Matthew clearly intended Matthew 27:52-53 to be understood as a historical claim, and since Licona claims that Matthew never intended that passage to be understood as a historical claim, then according to Licona's own standard, he is guility of denying biblical inerrancy.

On December 21, 2018, the *New York Times* put out an article titled "Professor, Was Jesus Really Born to a Virgin?" In this article, NYT author Nicholas Kristof interviewed William Lane Craig. At one point in the article, Kristof asked William Lane Craig about contradictions in the Bible, and he asked William Lane Craig why he and other christians insist on the concept of biblical inerrancy. William Lane Craig said the following in response:

"I don't insist on the inerrancy of Scripture. Rather, what I insist on is what C.S. Lewis called "mere Christianity," that is to say, the core doctrines of Christianity. Harmonizing perceived contradictions in the Bible is a matter of in-house discussion amongst Christians. What really matters are questions like: Does God exist? Are there objective moral values? Was Jesus truly God and truly man? How did his death on a Roman cross serve to overcome our moral wrongdoing and estrangement from God? These are, as one philosopher puts it, the "questions that matter," not how Judas died." (62)

When asked why he insists on biblical inerrancy,

William Lane Craig says that he doesn't insist on the inerrancy of scripture, and that the issue of contradictions in the Bible is an in-house debate among christians for christians to resolve. This is a soft denial of biblical inerrancy.

As someone who was once an old earth creationist before becoming a young earth creationist, I have seen old earth creationists like Frank Turek suggest that the issue of old versus young earth creationism is an in-house debate amongst Christians, and that we don't need to talk about it publically. This is a common response from old earth creationists when they are confronted with something that they feel they cannot refute, and this instance, we see William Lane Craig saying the same thing about contradictions in the Bible. This indicates to me that behind closed doors, William Lane Craig probably does believe that the Bible has errors in it in regards to history and science.

William Lane Craig is considered by many to be the best Christian apologist on planet earth, and yet when given a chance to stand for biblical inerrancy, William Lane Craig did a soft denial of biblical inerrancy. If William Lane Craig actually was the best apologist christianity has to offer, then our worldview would be in a heap of trouble. Fortunately for us, he isn't.

On January 15, 2018, old earth creationist blogger James Bishop published an article titled "Why I No Longer Hold To Inerrancy & The Need For A New Model Of Inspiration". Unfortunately, I could not find the original article that he wrote, but I do have a video response to this article on my BitChute channel titled "James Bishop Denies Biblical Inerrancy (Justin Derby)". In this video, we see James Bishop write the following:

"But the problem for conservative inerrant views of scripture is this: The Bible is not inerrant. In other words, the Bible really does make errors historically, morally, and scientifically, a view that took shape in me over the past four years." (63)

While most old earth creationists deny biblical inerrancy with their actions, or merely hint at it with their words, James Bishop is one of the few to come right and actually say pubically that the Bible has historical, scientific, and moral errors in it, and that he therefore rejects biblical inerrancy.

The thing that Mike Licona, William Lane Craig, and James Bishop all have in common is that they denied the straight-forward and contextual reading of the Bible on origins long before they denied biblical innerrancy. When you make the majority opininon of the scientific and academic community a higher authority than God and the Bible, not only will you reject what the Bible says on origins, but eventually you will start to reject other things that the Bible clearly teaches. After all, the same scientific and academic community that tells us that evolution and deep time is true also tells us that the Bible has all these historical, scientific, and moral errors in it.

Old earth creationism, when taken to its logical conclusion, leads to denial of biblical inerrancy.

OTHER HERESIES THAT OLD EARTH CREATIONISM TEACHES

There are other heresies that old earth creationism teaches in order to justify itself, and we're going to return to old earth creationist Frank Turek, who teaches these heresies.

When we return to Turek's article "Why Andy Stanley Is Right About The Foundation Of Christianity And How To Defend It", we find Turek writing the following:

"Let me sum up this important point in another way. The ontological foundation of Christianity is not a collection of ancient writings we call the Bible. The ontological foundation of Christianity is the reality of God and the historicity of the biblical events including the Resurrection of Christ. (In fact, the New Testament wouldn't exist unless the Resurrection occurred.) So while we need all of the Bible to more fully understand God and live the Christian life, we don't need all the Bible to understand its most important message—the Gospel."

Seriously, Frank Turek?! We don't need all of the Bible to fully understand the gospel message of salvation? What about what Jesus told his disciples when he appeared to them in Luke 24?

Luke 24:44-49: *"He said to them, 'This is what I told you while I was still with you: Everything must be fulfilled that is written about me in the Law of Moses, the Prophets and the Psalms.'*

Then he opened their minds so they could understand the Scriptures. He told them, 'This is what is written: The Messiah will suffer and rise from the dead on the third day, and repentance for the forgiveness of sins will be preached in his name to all nations, beginning at Jerusalem. You are witnesses of these things. I am going to send you what my Father has promised; but stay in the city until you have been clothed with power from on high.'"

As we can see from above, Jesus told his disciples that virtually the entire Old Testament wrote about him, and then he tells them that the gospel message of salvation is based on what the Old Testament scriptures say; Jesus is clearly teaching that you can't fully understand the gospel message of salvation without understanding the Old Testament, which means that you need all of the Bible to fully understand the gospel message of salvation.

Is Frank Turek even aware that he's contradicting the words of the one he claims to follow? Does he even care?

"That's Andy's approach because many in our culture believe that if you doubt one story in the Bible you can't believe any of it. Andy's apologetic approach defuses that erroneous belief and for good reason. Believing in Noah and Jonah are not essential to your salvation, but believing in the Resurrection is!" (64)

Well Frank Turek, the reason that so many people in our culture believe that you can't believe in any of the Bible if you doubt one story in the Bible is because Jesus himself taught the concept!

In John 3:10-12, we see Jesus say the following:

"'You are Israel's teacher,' said Jesus, 'and do you not understand these things? Very truly I tell you, we speak of what we know, and we testify to what we have seen, but still you people do not accept our testimony. I have spoken to you of earthly things and you do not believe; how then will you believe if I speak of heavenly things?'"

In John 3:12, Jesus taught that if you can't trust the Bible when it makes historical and scientific claims, then you can't trust gospel message of salvation; this same Jesus went on in his ministry to teach that Noah and Jonah are historical facts, so it turns out that believing in Noah and Jonah actually is essential to your salvation, every bit as much as the resurrection is.

Turek seems to have a nasty habit of directly contradicting the words of the Jesus that he claims to submit to, and in this particular case, he is saying that what Jesus taught in John 3:12 is an erroneous belief.

How many heresies does old earth creationism need to commit before christians in general acknowledge that old earth creationism is a heresy, and that old earth creationists are heretics?

FINAL THOUGHTS ON OLD EARTH CREATIONISM

As we can see from this chapter, old earth creationists are compromisers because they place "modern science" (which is actually modern secular science) as the ultimate authority on reality over the Bible. Old earth creationists are also heretics because the Bible clearly teaches a 6,000 year-old universe and Earth, and yet they teach that the universe and earth are billions of years old. They're also heretics because they teach a number of different heresies in order to try and prove that the Bible supports their worldview.

Old earth creationists seem to believe that if they reinterpret the Bible in light of evolution, deep time, and big bang cosmology in order to mesh the atheistic evolutionary worldview together with the Bible, this will somehow convince unbelievers to become Christians. They couldn't be more wrong.

On December 30, 2019, Styxhexenhammer666, an independent media analyst with over 482,000 subscribers to his YouTube channel and over 134,000 subscribers to his BitChute channel, put out a video on his BitChute channel titled "Mormon "Church" May Have Embezzled 100 Billion in 20 Years (Bitchute Exclusive)". It is in this video where we see Styx say the following:

"It's interesting how that happens with religions. They continuously revise themselves, and they revise what their own leaders said or did according with modern standards of what is or is not considered acceptable or objectively true. So it's like, 'oh, the Bible doesn't teach against evolution! Just ignore the whole 6,000 year-old earth thing, just ignore Noah's ark, just ignore the fact that putting stripes on a piece of wood does not make goats stripey. Ignore all of the weird S--- in there. Perfectly fine. Don't worry, God was the first scientist!' It's, like, no, not really, but you know, ok. It's cute. It's cute to watch the cop-outs" (65)

As someone who has been subscribed to Styx's BitChute channel since 2017 and consistently watches his videos related to news and politics, tech censorship, and occasionally his religious videos, I have seen Styx admit that he does not know if there is a God out there or not, and that he doesn't care enough about the issue to figure it out. I also know that Styx used to associate himself with the atheist/skeptic community on YouTube before most of them sold out to the far-leftist authoritarians. Clearly, Styx is not a Christian, or a young earth creationist, and because he believes in evolution, deep time, and big bang cosmology, I think it would be fair to classify him as an evolutionist.

With that in mind, it should be an eye-opener for old earth creationists to see someone like Styx look at the Bible and acknowledge that it teaches that the earth and universe are 6,000 years old when it is read in a straight-forward and contextual manner. It's also an eye-opener to see someone like Styx laugh at old earth creationists for trying to reinterpret the Bible in light of his worldview. Someone like Styx represents your average atheist and agnostic, so if his response is any indicator, atheists and agnostics are not impressed when old earth creationists try to reinterpret the Bible in light of evolution, billions of years, and big bang cosmology; it does not even come close to convincing them to convert to the biblical worldview.

When old earth creationists reinterpret the Bible in light of evolution, deep time, and big bang cosmology, what they are communicating with their actions is that they think that God is the worst communicator of all time. That's the message you send when you claim that God made everything over billions of years, but wrote his written word to humanity in such a way that it teaches that God made everything over six ordinary days roughly 6,000 years ago.

Atheist & evolutionist YouTubers like Viced Rhino and Paulogia capitalize off of this and claim that the Bible must not be written very clearly if old earth creationists and young earth creationists cannot even agree with what the Bible says on origins.

I have often heard old earth creationists claim that young earth creationism makes the God of the Bible out to be a deceptive god because God made reality with the appearance of billions of years of age even though he made everything 6,000 years ago.

The fact of the matter is that by claiming that God

made everything over the course of billions of years before writing his written word in such a way that it says that God made everything over six days roughly 6,000 years ago when read in a straight-forward and contextual manner, the god of old earth creationism is the one who is a deceptive god.

Old earth creationists will respond to this by saying that the people God was revealing his revelations to were just too ignorant and stupid to comprehend that God made everything over billions of years, so he wrote his written word in such a way so as to communicate that God made everything over the course of six days roughly 6,000 years ago in order to dumb things down for the audience of the time. God was apparently counting on old earth creationists to come along in the future and properly reinterpret his coded message in order to arrive at the proper understanding that God made everything over the course of billions of years.

So the God of old earth creationism deceived us with the way he wrote his written word to us because we were too stupid at the time to comprehend the idea of him making everything over billions of years. That totally makes me want to convert back to old earth creationism! Not!

The completely disregard of and disrespect for God and his

written word that is displayed by old earth creationists, people who claim to be Bible believers and followers of Jesus, makes them a bigger threat to the biblical worldview than atheists and evolutionists could ever be.

Conclusion

If you have reached this point in the book, you have taken in a lot of information regarding young earth creationism, atheistic evolution, and old earth creationism.

You have seen all the evidence that shows that the Bible teaches a 6,000 year-old earth and universe, and that young earth creationism is a salvation issue. You have seen all the evidence that shows that the atheistic evolutionary worldview is an anti-science religion whose adherents project themselves onto Christians and creationists in order to condemn them. You have also seen that old earth creationism is rank heresy that relies on several other heresies in order to justify itself, all of which leads to the biggest compromise ever on the biblical worldview.

It's also possible that even after reading and seeing all of this, you might still disagree with me about young earth creationism being the hill to die on. If that is what you are thinking, then what you need to realize is that I'm not the only one who thinks that young earth creationism is the hill to die on. The globalist establishment agrees with me.

On July 13, 2017, *USA Today* put out an article titled "Creationism support is at a new low. The reason should give us hope." In this article, *USA Today* essentially gives the thumbs up to theistic evolution by commending organizations like *BioLogos* for meshing the atheistic evolutionary worldview and the biblical worldview together by reinterpreting the Bible in light of the atheistic evolutionary worldview. It is in the last three paragraphs of the article where we read the following:

"These tea leaves tell us that more people are refusing the all-or-nothing choice between faith and science and opting instead for a third way: Acceptance of the overwhelming scientific evidence for evolution while seeing a divine role in the process. "Divine evolution" is a term some use for it.

If we were to apply this approach to other stalemated arguments and false binaries, what other possibilities might emerge? Can't we support Black Lives Matter and police officers who serve conscientiously? Can't we support the legal availability of abortion and strategies that would reduce its incidence? Can't we accept the scientific consensus on climate change and acknowledge a role for free-market business innovation as part of the solution? In the ongoing tussle over health care, can't we envision a system that combines the best private and government solutions?

For now, something to appreciate: Growing public rejection of an unhelpful creationism-vs.-evolution fight that does no favors for either religion or science. As more believers are wisely accepting, you can embrace both — and both are better for it." (66)

As we can see from the conclusion of their article, *USA Today* is saying that if Christians are willing to compromise on the creation versus evolution debate by reinterpreting the Bible in light of evolution, deep time, and big bang cosmology in order to create theistic evolution, then Christians should be willing to accept the Black Lives Matter and ANTIFA movements, abortion, the LGBTQ movement, the bogus climate change narrative being pushed by the globalists and United Nations, and anything else that the globalist establishment tells them to accept.

In other words, if you accept and believe in the young earth creationism timeline of history as well as the rest of the biblical worldview, then you have every logical reason and grounds to reject the entire far-leftist authoritarian and globalist agenda.

But if you compromise and you reinterpret the Bible in

light of evolution, billions of years, and big bang cosmology, then you have zero logical reasons or grounds to reject any part of the far-leftist authoritarian and globalist agenda.

Young earth creationism is literally the hill to die on.

INTERNET CENSORSHIP OF YOUNG EARTH CREATIONISM IS COMING

With all the massive censorship of conservatives, Trump supporters, and alternative media personalities and organizations on the mainstream internet going on the last couple years, and the minimal at best censorship of young earth creationism content, there is a temptation on the part of young earth creationists to think that they won't be the victims of internet censorship in the future.

I'm here to warn you that young earth creationists getting censored off the mainstream internet is a matter of when, not if.

On January 25, The YouTube Team put out a blog post on the official YouTube blog titled " Continuing our work to improve recommendations on YouTube". It is in this post where we read the following:

"We'll continue that work this year, including taking a closer look at how we can reduce the spread of content that comes close to—but doesn't quite cross the line of—violating our Community Guidelines. To that end, we'll begin reducing recommendations of borderline content and content that could misinform users in harmful ways—such as videos promoting a phony miracle cure for a serious illness, claiming the earth is flat, or making blatantly false claims about historic events like 9/11." (67)

As you can see, back in January of 2019, YouTube promised that they were going to censor flat earth content by reducing the amount of times that flat earth videos show up in the recommended videos sections of people's YouTube feeds as well as reduce the amount of times that flat earth videos show up on the side bar of YouTube videos. In the time that has passed since this announcement, YouTube kept true to the word, and flat earth content has seen a dramatic reduction in traffic as a result of this artifical suppression.

Now I am not a flat-earther, nor will I ever be because to be a flat earther would require me to deny the existence of outer space, and I can't do that, but I do know that there is overlap between the young earth and flat earth community. By that, I mean that there are young earth creationists out there who are also flat earthers. I know this is true because

I've had such people comment on my videos in the past.

If sites like YouTube are willing to censor flat earth content, then it is only a matter of time before they start censoring young earth creationism content. Independent media analyst Tim Pool came to the same conclusion when he put out a video on January 25, 2019 titled " MAJOR CHANGE TO YOUTUBE Will Impact Alternative Media" on his BitChute channel. It is in this video where you hear Tim Pool say the following:

"Is YouTube going to start determining where certain religous views are not acceptable because historians disagree with them? Think about the issue here.

Earth is flat. Ok, I think that's ridiculous, but imagine this: People who are Christian, who are Muslim, believe the earth is only several thousand years old. Not all of them, but many of them do because the Bible basically says as such, basically. Well scientists disagree. They believe that carbon-dating says the earth is much, much older than that. I believe the scientific community. I am not a religious person. I am also not going to tell a religious person what they can or cannot believe.

If someone makes videos saying, 'I am going to explain to you why the earth is only 5,000 years old,' is YouTube going to remove that recommendation because, like flat earth, it's just proven false by the science community? This is dangerous to free expression. YouTube, you cannot be in the business of determining what people are allowed to believe!

Flat earth is ridiculous; you have every right to think it's true! If YouTube gets into this business, they will come to a point of actually suppressing religious content as well. What if you don't believe in evolution? Fox News ran a segment, like, a few weeks ago where they said evolution wasn't true. I absolutely disagree with that! I think it's wrong, and I think it's irresponsible, but I also think they have freedom of expression, speech, and religion in this country." (68)

As we can see, Tim Pool is an evolutionist and a non-believer, but even he recognizes the danger of YouTube censoring flat earthers, and he acknowledges that the next group YouTube will censor after flat earthers is the young earth creationist community. As we can also see from his words, Tim Pool is not a fan of young earth creationists getting censored on the internet.

The reason why the mainstream internet is not doing a mass purging of young earth creationism content as well as young earth creatinionists is because right now they busy censoring the alternative media as well as independent content creators who cover news and politics. These are the people with a lot of reach who would be the first to report on mainstream sites censoring young earth creationists, so YouTube is working on muzzling them first. Make no mistake though, when the time comes, mainstream internet censorship will turn its attention to the young earth creationism community.

WHAT CAN WE DO NOW?

Now that you know the truth about young earth creationism, atheistic evolution, and old earth creationism, what you need to do is follow the biblical command to engage in apologetics, and you need to make the truth about young earth creationism, atheistic evolution, and old earth creationism known to the world.

We are commanded as followers of Jesus and adherents to the biblical worldview to defend the truthfulness of the biblical worldview. As 1 Peter 3:15 says:

"...Always be prepared to give an answer to everyone who asks you to give the reason for the hope that you have. But do this with gentleness and respect..."

The word "reason" in this passage is the modern english translation of the Greek word apologia, which is where we get the term "apologetics" from. So in 1 Peter 3:15, we are literally commanded as followers of Jesus to give an intellectual defense of the biblical worldview, meaning that we need to provided evidence that it is true.

In relation to young earth creationism, we need to provide the evidence that young earth creationism is true, as I have tried to do in this book.

We are also commanded as followers of Jesus and adherents to the biblical worldview to debunk all other worldviews because they stand in opposition to the biblical worldview. In 2 Corinthians 10:5, we read the following:

"We demolish arguments and every pretension that sets itself up against the knowledge of God, and we take captive every thought to make it obedient to Christ."

As we can see, we are commanded by God to demolish every argument and pretension that sets itself up against the knowledge of God. Since all other worldviews set themselves up against the knowledge of God that is contained in the biblical worldview, this means that Christians are commanded by God to debunk all other worldviews. That is the second half of God's call for us to engage in apologetics.

While you are welcome to speak the truth about young earth creationism, atheistic evolution, and old earth creationism on the mainstream internet, the mainstream internet is rapidly becoming a less viable place to do so due to their censorious ways.

If you are going to engage in apologetics on the internet, the best place to do it is on alternative technology social media platforms that champion freedom of speech. I'm talking about platforms like JoshWho TV, UGETube, NewTube, Pocketnet, Loop, USA.Life, BitChute, Gab, Minds, and others. In the resource section at the back of this book, I include a list of alt-tech platforms that I am on so that you can find a lot of these alt-tech platforms and use them for yourself.

I believe that if Christians start accepting the young earth creationism timeline of history that the Bible teaches, and they starting recognizing and acknowledging old earth creationism for the heresy that is, we can not only have an easier time refuting the atheistic evolutionary worldview, but we can clear out a lot of the intellectual obstacles that prevent people from accepting the gospel of Jesus Christ.

The foundations of the biblical worldview are under attack from the outside as well as from within, and nothing gets more foundational than the biblical worldview's explanation of origins. We cannot compromise with a bunch of people who hate God, and who have no respect for his word. We have to stand strong on what the Bible says, and when the world comes down on us to condemn us for not believing in evolution, deep time, and big bang cosmology, there is only one thing that we need to do.

Don't flinch.

End Notes

1. Barr, James. Letter to David C. C. Watson, April 23, 1984.

2. Davis, Jud. "24 Hours—Plain as Day" *Answers In Genesis*. 1 April 2012. Web. 11 August 2019. <https://answersingenesis.org/days-of-creation/24-hours-plain-as-day/>

3. Friel, Todd. *Judge Not*. Apple Valley, Minnesota: Burning Bush Communications, 2015. Print.

4. Lawrence, Dr. Troy. *Origins*. Lawrence Publishing, 2017. Print

5. Morris, John D. "Earth's Magnetic Field" *Institute For Creation Research*. 1 August 2010. Web. 21 October 2019. <https://www.icr.org/article/earths-magnetic-field>

6. Flank, Lenny. "Creationists And 'Magnetic Field Decay'". *Debunking Creationism AKA "Intelligent Design"*. 1995. Web. 3 January 2020. <http://huecotanks.com/debunk/magnetic.htm >

7. Brill, Richard C. "Is it true that the strength of the Earth's magnetic field is decreasing? What's the effect?" *Scientific American*. 5 October 1998. Web. 3 January 2020. <https://www.scientificamerican.com/article/is-it-true-that-the-stren/>

8. Fuentes, Johnathan. "6 Horrible Consequences of Earth Losing its Magnetic Field". Futurism. 25 February 2015. Web. 3 January 2020. <https://futurism.com/6-horrible-consequences-earth-losing-magnetic-field>

9. Yeoman, Barry. "Schwietzer's Dangerous Discovery". Discover. 26 April 2006. Web. 19 January 2020. <https://www.discovermagazine.com/the-sciences/schweitzers-dangerous-discovery>

10. Peake, Tracey. "Iron Preserves, Hides Ancient Tissues in Fossilized Remains". NC State University News. 26 November 2013. Web. 19 January 2020. <https://news.ncsu.edu/2013/11/schweitzer-iron/>

11. Armitage, Mark H., and Anderson, Kevin Lee. "Soft sheets of fibrillar bone from a fossil of the supraorbital horn of the dinosaur Triceratops horridus". *Acta Histochemica*. Vol. 115. No. 6. 2013. Pp. 603-608.

12. "Lawsuit: CSUN Scientist Fired After Soft Tissue Found On Dinosaur Fossil". CBS Los Angeles. 24 July 2014. Web. 1 July 2020. <https://archive.vn/KWH4F>

13. Horton, Ashley. "Former CSUN employee receives legal settlement from the university". The Sundial. 11 November 2016. Web. 1 July 2020. <https://archive.vn/If4Of>

14. Futuyma, Douglas. Science On Trial: The Case For Evolution. New York: Pantheon Books. 1983. P. 197

15. Dawkins, Richard. *The Blind Watchmaker*. W.W. Norton & Company: New York, USA. Print. 1986. P. 229

16. Mitchell, J.D. *The Creation Dialogues*. Gresham, Oregon: CEC Publications. 2014. Print.

17. Mayr, Ernst. "Darwin's Influence On Modern Thought". 24 November 2009. Web. 31 August 2020. <https://archive.vn/9rlzD>

18. Mayr, Ernst. Interview with Edge. <https://archive.vn/iMFJX>

19. Pickrell, John. "Introduction: Evolution". New Scientist. 4 September 2006. Web. 6 September 2020. <https://archive.vn/Mcqfy>

20. "What Is Microevolution?" Understanding Evolution. Web. 6 September 2020. <https://archive.vn/SqCQC>

21. "What Is Macroevolution?" Understanding Evolution. Web. 6 September 2020. <https://archive.vn/iu97X>

22. "Introduction To Human Evolution". Smithsonian National Museum of Natural History. Web. 6 September 2020. <https://archive.vn/9SUq9>

23. Professor Stick. "Antibiotic Resistance Is Apparently Not Evolution." Online Video Clip. *YouTube*. YouTube. 7 July 2018. 7:29. Web. 8 September 2020. <https://youtu.be/4A_pCbFr7AI>

24. Darwin, Charles. *On the origin of species by means of natural selection, or the preservation of favoured races in the struggle for life.* London: Murray. 1859. Web. <https://archive.vn/bO2Td>

25. McIntyre, Donald B. & McKirrdy, A. *James Hutton: The Founder Of Modern Geology.* National Museums of Scotland. Print. 2006. P. 1

26. Royal Society of Edinsburgh. *The Royal Society Of Edinsburgh Volume 5*. Arkrose Press. Print. 1805, P. 71-73

27. Marcy, Milt. *The Emperors Who Had No Clothes*. Create Space Publishing. Print. 2013. P. 75

28. *Life, Letters, and Journals Of Sir Charles Lyell, Bart*. Sagwan Press. Print. 2015. P. 271

29. See Footnote 27, P. 105

30. Gould, Stephen Jay. "Evolution As Fact And Theory" The Unofficial Stephen Jay Gould Archive. May 1981. Web. 12 October 2020. <https://archive.vn/WvYt6>

31. Eddington, A.S., "The Nature of the Physical World," [1928], The Gifford Lectures 1927, Cambridge University Press: Cambridge UK, 1933, reprint, pp.74-75.

32. See footnote 15, P. 1

33. Professor Stick. "Another Creationist Claims The Universe Was Created." Online Video Clip. *YouTube*. YouTube. 24 June 2017. 0:36. Web. 13 October 2020. <https://youtu.be/geUo-Tm51k8>

34. Todd, Scott C. "A view from kansas on that evolution debate." Nature. 30 September 1999. Web. 14 October 2020. <https://archive.vn/BZaGU>

35. Gjersoe, Nathalia. "Evolution Makes Scientific Sense. So Why Do Many People Reject It?" The Guardian. 31 March 2016. Web. 15 October 2020. <https://archive.vn/Q9YRZ>

36. Theodosius Dobzhansky. "ON METHODS OF EVOLUTIONARY BIOLOGY AND ANTHROPOLOGY: Part I. Biology". *American Scientist*. 45, 388, 1957. Web. 3 November 2020. <https://www.jstor.org/stable/27826983?read-now=1&seq=9#page_scan_tab_contents>

37. C. Leon Harris. "An Axiomatic Interpretation of the Neo-Darwinian Theory of Evolution". *Perspectives In Biology And Medicine*. 18, 2, Winter 1975. P. 183

38. Professor Stick. "Creationist Debunks New Evidence Of Abiogenesis." Online Video Clip. *YouTube*. YouTube. 27 September 2020. 1:33. Web. 13 October 2020. <https://youtu.be/soqroZVIcZw>

39. See Footnote 37, 5:03

40. Professor Stick. "More Creationist Arguments Against

The Big Bang." Online Video Clip. *YouTube*. YouTube. 17 March 2019. 4:42. Web. 13 October 2020. <https://youtu.be/4iAxhYaf_rU>

41. Shannon Q. "Hate Preach The Next Generation." Online Video Clip. *YouTube*. YouTube. 7 June 2019. 16:54. Web. 14 October 2020. <https://youtu.be/GihkCSyJkxY>

42. Shannon Q. "Ken Ham donates over $4000 to LGBT charity! Paulogia and Shannon Q Celebration!." Online Video Clip. *YouTube*. YouTube. 18 August 2019. 4:03. Web. 14 October 2020. <https://youtu.be/fbtknYoQWzg>

43. Paulogia. "Atheist Banned From Ken Ham Event (Paulogia Denied)." Online Video Clip. *YouTube*. YouTube. 13 April 2018. 6:29. Web. 14 October 2020. <https://youtu.be/nDpXNjhqoko>

44. "Top U.S. creationist's invitation as keynote speaker for Alberta homeschooling convention draws fire". *CBC News*. 8 November 2017. Web. 14 October 2020. <https://archive.vn/dtsLR>

45. See footnote 43, 7:21

46. Scott, Eugenie. "Monkey Business." *The Sciences*.

January/February 1996. Print. P. 25

47. Gish, Duane. *Winning The Creation Debate.* El Canjon, California: Institute For Creation Research. 2002. Print. P. 5

48. Nye, Bill. "Bill Nye's Take On The Nye-Ham Debate." Skeptical Inquirer. May/June 2014. Web. 14 October 2020. <https://archive.vn/ci4wT>

49. Witham, Larry A. *Where Darwinism Meets The Bible.* Oxford University Press, USA. 2002. Print. P. 23

50. Zivkovic, Bora. "Why Teaching Evolution Is Dangerous". *ScienceBlogs.com.* 25 August 2008. Web. 19 August 2014. <https://archive.vn/6mINy>

51. Cambridge Dictionary. "Compromise". Web. 16 October 2020. <https://dictionary.cambridge.org/dictionary/english/compromise>

52. Licona, Mike. *When The Saints Go Marching In (Matthew 27:52-53): Historicity, Apocalyptic Symbol, and Biblical Inerrancy.* 2011. P. 9-10. Online. <http://www.risenjesus.com/wp-content/uploads/2011-eps-saints-paper.pdf>

53. Lutzer, Erwin W. *7 Reasons Why You Can Trust The Bible*. Moody Publishers, 2015. Print. P. 160.

54. TTOR. "Debunking William Lane Craig's Arguments Against YEC (Justin Derby)." Online Video Clip. *BitChute*. BitChute. 29 August 2018. 1:40. Web. 22 September 2020. <https://www.bitchute.com/video/qwc1g3myVhsQ/>

55. Turek, Frank. "Why Andy Stanley Is Right About The Foundation Of Christianity And How To Defend It". *Cross Examined*. 8 September 2016. Web. 11 June 2017. <http://crossexamined.org/andy-stanley-right-foundation-christianity-defend/>

56. Frank Turek. "How Old Is The Universe?". Online Video Clip. *YouTube*. YouTube. 28 December 2015. 5:12. Web. 6 November 2020. <https://youtu.be/TqMwqwb8Vno>

57. See Footnote 54, 15:54

58. Marshall, Perry. *Evolution 2.0*. Dallas, Texas: BenBella Books. 2015. Print. P. 327

59. See footnote 3

60. Grigg, Russell M. (1996). "Naming the animals: all in a

day's work for Adam." *Creation*, 18(4). Web. <http://creation.com/naming-the-animals-all-in-a-day-s-work-for-adam>

61. See footnote 52

62. Kristof, Nicholas. "Professor, Was Jesus Really Born to a Virgin?" *New York Times*. 21 December 2018. Web. 19 October 2020. <https://archive.vn/koQ26>

63. TTOR. "James Bishop Denies Biblical Inerrancy (Justin Derby)." Online Video Clip. *BitChute*. BitChute. 21 January 2018. 1:48. Web. 19 October 2020. <https://www.bitchute.com/video/nlEILysGI3gK/>

64. See footnote 55

65. Styxhexenhammer666. "Mormon "Church" May Have Embezzled 100 Billion in 20 Years (Bitchute Exclusive)." Online Video Clip. *BitChute*. BitChute. 30 December 2019. 9:05. Web. 19 October 2020. <https://www.bitchute.com/video/Clf6dEBpTwVo/>

66. Krattenmaker, Tom. "Creationism support is at a new low. The reason should give us hope." *USA Today*. 13 July 2017. Web. 19 October 2020. <https://archive.vn/KIKPL>

67. The YouTube Team. "Continuing our work to improve recommendations on YouTube." YouTube Official Blog. 25 January 2019. Web. 19 October 2020. <https://archive.vn/9DdKW>

68. Tim Pool. "MAJOR CHANGE TO YOUTUBE Will Impact Alternative Media." Online Video Clip. *BitChute*. BitChute. 25 January 2019. 4:15. Web. 19 October 2020. <https://www.bitchute.com/video/Qm-Jvy4oMoE/>

Resources

My Alt-Tech Presences

If you want to follow Justin on alternative technology social media platforms that champion freedom of speech, you can find Justin at the following places:

-CreationSocial: https://creation.social/page/view/15

-BitChute: https://www.bitchute.com/channel/ttor/

-JoshWho TV:
https://www.joshwhotv.com/channel/5d649488bbe53

-UGETube: https://videos.utahgunexchange.com/@TTOR

-NewTube: https://newtube.app/user/TTOR

-Loop: https://loop.joshwho.net/members/2442920

-USA.Life: https://usa.life/truththeobjectivereality

-Xephula: https://xephula.com/TTOR

-MAGABook: https://www.magabook.com/TTOR_Official

-Gorf: https://gorf.social/ttor

-BrighteonSocial: https://brighteon.social/@TTOR

-Gab: https://gab.com/TTOR

-Minds:
https://www.minds.com/Truth_The_Objective_Reality/

INERRANCY OF SCRIPTURES

If you would like to investigate the inerrancy of scripture topic a little deeper, then check out the following:

-*The Down-Grade Controversy* by Charles Spurgeon

-*The Battle for The Bible* by Harold Lindsell

-*The Great Evangelical Disaster* by Francis A. Schaeffer

--*Fatal Drift: Is The Church Losing Its Anchor?* by Dr. Jim Jenkins

Books On Young Earth Creationism:

-*Origins* by Dr. Troy Lawrence

-*The Creation Dialogues* by Dr. J.D Mitchell

-*Fossils: Description & Interpretation* by Dr. J.D Mitchell

-*Young Earth Science & The Dawn Of A New Worldview* by Jay Hall

-*Is A Young Earth Possible?* By Jay Hall

-*The Emperors Who Had No Clothes* by Milt Marcy

-*Secrets Of The Ica Stones And Nazca Lines* by Dennis Swift

-*Refuting Compromise* by Dr. Jonathan Sarfati

-*The Dark Side Of Charles Darwin* by Jerry Bergman

-*Slaughter Of The Dissidents* by Jerry Bergman

-*Silencing The Darwin Skeptics* by Jerry Bergman

-*Censoring The Darwin Skeptics* by Jerry Bergman

Quality Young Earth Creationist Ministries:

If you want to follow a legit ministry, I would check out the following sources:

-*Wretched TV* (Go here: http://www.wretchedradio.com/)

-*Reasons for Faith Ministries* (go here: http://kindell.nwcreation.net/index.htm)

-*Creation Engineering Concepts* (go here: https://www.creationengineeringconcepts.org/)

-*Northwest Creation Network* (YouTube channel: https://www.youtube.com/c/nwcreationnetwork)

-*Apologetics Forum Of Snohomish County* (Go here: https://www.apologeticsforum.org/)

-*Design Science Association* (Go here: http://designsciencenw.org/)

-*Adam's Lost Dream* (Go here: https://adamslostdream.blogspot.com/)

-*Piltdown Superman* (Go here: https://www.piltdownsuperman.com/)

Author Bio

Justin Derby is a Christian apologist who runs the apologetics ministry called *Truth: The Objective Reality*, and is a member of the International Association for Creation (IAC). Justin also runs the TTOR BitChute channel, which has over 2,200 subscribers, and is one of the top-600 channels on BitChute in terms of subscribers and total video views according to statchute.xyz

Justin also runs an alternative technology social media platform called CreationSocial, which serves as an alternative to Facebook. Justin is the author of *Another Inconvenient Truth: What Secular America Hates*. He graduated from Linfield College in the spring of 2013 with a degree in mass communication. Justin is available for guest speaking, and can be contacted through his ministry website at https://ttor.faithlifesites.com/.